Praise for Antony Lewis

"Einstein said t... ... ...
you don't unde... ...
clearly understa... ...
cryptocurrencie... ...
—Colin Platt, Cohost of *Blockchain Insider* podcast
& DLT/cryptocurrency researcher

"The first book that I've seen that really breaks
down concepts. An excellent insight into the key
concepts and real-world implications of bitcoin
and blockchain."
—Zennon Kapron, managing director
of Kapronasia

"If you want a book that over-sells blockchain, go
elsewhere. This explains the fundamentals clearly and
cuts through the hype."
—Richard Gendal Brown, CTO, R3

BITCOIN
ON THE GO

BITCOIN ON THE GO

The Basics of Bitcoins and Blockchains—Condensed

Based on the work of

ANTONY LEWIS

By the editors at Mango Publishing

CORAL GABLES

For permission requests, please contact the publisher at:
Mango Publishing Group
2850 S Douglas Road, 4th Floor
Coral Gables, FL 33134 USA
info@mango.bz

For special orders, quantity sales, course adoptions and corporate sales, please email the publisher at sales@mango.bz. For trade and wholesale sales, please contact Ingram Publisher Services at customer.service@ingramcontent.com or +1.800.509.4887.

Bitcoin on the Go: The Basics of Bitcoins and Blockchains—Condensed

Library of Congress Cataloging-in-Publication number: 2022944395
ISBN: (print) 978-1-68481-203-5 (ebook) 978-1-68481-204-2
BISAC category code: BUS090030, BUSINESS & ECONOMICS / E-Commerce / Online Trading

Printed in the United States of America

Table of Contents

INTRODUCTION

Bitcoin, blockchains, and cryptocurrencies are
fascinating to me because there are so many elements
to understand. This multidisciplinary nature is one of
the reasons I, and so many others, love the industry—
it is easy to get sucked into the rabbit hole, and as
you try to understand each element, every answer
begets more questions. The journey starts with 'What
is Bitcoin?' but the explanations and answers come
from the disciplines of economics, law, computer
science, finance, civil society, history, geopolitics, and
more. You could create a pretty comprehensive high
school curriculum around Bitcoin and have plenty of
material to spare.

And this is the very reason why it is so hard to
explain. This book is an attempt to cover the basics.
It is aimed at the thinking person but assumes that
the reader doesn't have a detailed background in the
various disciplines mentioned previously. Different
people will find different parts interesting. I try to

use analogies where I think they help explain some concepts, but be gentle with me: all analogies break down if stretched too far. And although I have tried to be accurate, there will still be oversimplifications, errors and omissions. What is true today may not be tomorrow: the pace of change is rapid. I am the first to admit that there are limits to my own technical expertise. Nevertheless, I hope that every reader comes away learning something new.

With so many cryptocurrencies, it is not easy to make accurate generalisations: there are bound to be exceptions. For example, Bitcoin has "proof-of-work" (which we will cover later). This competition consumes a lot of electricity. However, not all cryptocurrencies work this way.

Bearing this in mind, we will start with how Bitcoin works and then discuss some differences between Bitcoin and other cryptocurrencies.

Chapter 1

BITCOIN BASICS

People refer to Bitcoin as a digital currency, virtual currency, or cryptocurrency, but it may be easier to think of it as an electronic asset. Bitcoin is also sometimes described as a digital token, and in some respects that is accurate, but the term token is now also used to mean something more specific, so the ambiguity of this term is best avoided.

What Are Bitcoins?

Bitcoins are digital assets ("coins") whose ownership is recorded on an electronic ledger updated (almost) simultaneously on about ten thousand independently operated computers, known as "nodes," around the world. This ledger is called Bitcoin's blockchain. Each node independently validates all pending transactions wherever they arise. Specialist nodes, called miners, bundle valid transactions into blocks and distribute those blocks to nodes across the network.

Anyone can buy bitcoins, own them, and send them to others. Every Bitcoin transaction is shared publicly in plain text on Bitcoin's blockchain. Anyone can, in theory, create bitcoins for themselves too. This is part of the block creation process, called mining, and is described later.

What Is the Point of Bitcoin?

The purpose of Bitcoin is described in a short document written by a pseudonymous Satoshi Nakamoto, published in October 2008. The abstract says:

> *A purely peer-to-peer version of electronic cash would allow online payments to be sent directly...without going through a financial institution.... We propose a solution...using a peer-to-peer network.*

It sets out the purpose of Bitcoin and how Bitcoin derives both value and utility. As popularised by cryptocurrency industry commentator Tim Swanson, Bitcoin is designed as censorship-resistant digital cash.

How Does Bitcoin Work?

The Bitcoin blockchain is managed by about ten thousand computers. The most used software is called "Bitcoin Core," and the source code to this software is published on GitHub. This software contains the full range of functionalities needed for the network to exist. It can perform the following tasks:

- Connect with other participants in the Bitcoin network

- Download the blockchain from other participants

- Store the blockchain

- Listen for new transactions

- Validate those transactions

- Store those transactions

- Relay valid transactions to other nodes

- Listen for new blocks

- Validate those blocks

- Store those blocks as part of its blockchain

- Relay valid blocks

- Create new blocks

- "Mine" new blocks

- Manage addresses

- Create and send transactions

However, in practice, the software is usually only used for its bookkeeping function, as explained in this section.

Bitcoin: an electronic payment system without a financial institution. If parties need to identify themselves, they lose privacy and are vulnerable to interference, coercion, prison, or worse. Every single part of the solution needs to work with these constraints in mind.

The solution starts with a classic centralised model and then tries to decentralise it, building the design of Bitcoin step by step.

Classic Centralised Model

Let's start with a list with two columns: Account and Balance, managed by an administrator.

Classic centralized model

Bookkeeper	
Account	Balance
000001	$100

000002	$50
000003	$240

The administrator assigns account numbers to customers, who make payments by instructing the administrator. Each customer is named and, for security, has a password linked to their account.

Account mapping

Account	Username	Pin/Password
000001	Alice	1234
000002	Bob	8888
000003	Charlie	9876

The administrator maintains the central record of balances and makes all payments. They also ensure no one spends money they don't have.

But if we want anyone to transact with anyone else without censorship, we need to remove the administrator, starting with anyone being able to open an account without needing permission from the administrator.

Problems and Solutions

Problem: Accounts Need Permission

The administrator's job is to assign you an unused account number, then set you up with a username and password so that the administrator knows you are making the request.

The administrator grants permission to open the account and may refuse that permission. At that point, you have a point of third-party control.

Is there a way you can open an account without having to ask permission? Well, cryptography provides a solution.

Solution: Use Public Keys as Account Numbers

Instead of names or account numbers and passwords, why not use addresses as account numbers and digital signatures instead of passwords?

Addresses are mathematically derived from public keys. By using addresses as account numbers, anyone can create an account with their computer.

Using user-generated addresses instead of accounts

Bookkeeper	
Address (derived from public key)	Balance
1mk41QrLLeC9Cwph6UgV4GZ5nRfejQFsS	$100
1Lna1HnAZ5nuGyyTjPWqh34KxERCYLeEM1	$50
1PFZiJCYYaWc1C2FCc2UWXDU197rhyP	$240

You can tell the world this Bitcoin address to allow people to pay to it. No one can spend anything from it unless they have the private key, which only you have.

Could someone else already be using an address that you randomly picked? Possible, but unlikely. Bitcoin's scheme uses a random number between 0 and 115,792,089,237,316,195,423, 570,985,008,687,907,853,269,984,665,640,564,039,457,584,007,913,129,639,935 as a private key. There are so many private keys available that the possibility of stumbling across someone else's account is virtually nil. As one commentator said, "Go back to bed and don't worry about this ever happening."

Public/private key pairs also solve the authentication problem. You digitally sign the transaction with your private key. The receiver can then check that the digital signature is valid for the respective account number.

No more usernames and passwords or account mapping

Account	Username	Pin/Password
000001	~~Ai~~	1234
000002	~~Bob~~	8888
000003	Claire	9876

Problem: Single Central Bookkeeper

We still have the third-party administrator in the role of central bookkeeper, and it would be classified as a financial institution, who must identify you and all other customers, known as Know Your Customer or KYC. It can also be coerced to censor transactions.

So, for a digital cash system resistant to third-party influence, including control and censorship, we need to remove that single point of control.

Single bookkeeper: Not censorship resistant

Bookkeeper	
Address (derived from public key)	Balance
1mk41QrLLeC9Cwph6UgV4GZ5nRfejQFsS	$100
1Lna1HnAZ5nuGyyTjPWqh34KxERCYLeEM1	$50
1PFZip1iJCYYaWc1C2FCc2UWXDU197rhyP	$240

Solution: Replicate the Books

The solution to the central point of control problem is for anyone anywhere to become a bookkeeper. All bookkeepers maintain the same complete records and have equal seniority.

Replicated bookkeeping

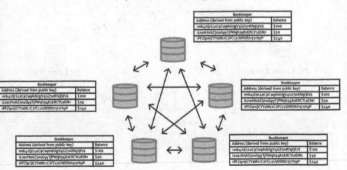

In Bitcoin, any individual with a computer, adequate storage, and internet bandwidth can download some software (or write their own), connect to a few neighbours, and become a bookkeeper.

Problem: Transaction Ordering

Hundreds of transactions can be created anywhere in the world. If every bookkeeper tried to put these transactions in order, there would be many conflicting orders.

Transaction (Tx) ordering problem in distributed network

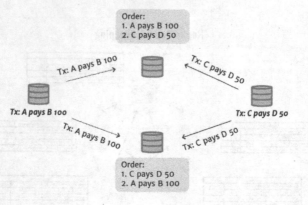

How do we get an agreed ordering of transactions?

Solution: Blocks

We can instead record transactions in batches, page by page instead of transaction by transaction. Individual transactions can be passed around the network, then entered into the books in less frequent batches, called blocks.

Bundle transactions into blocks that are created less frequently

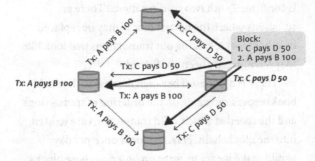

Blocks likely reach all bookkeepers in the network before another one is created. This means that a bookkeeper now performs two functions:

1. Validating and propagating "pending" transactions

2. Validating, storing, and propagating blocks of transactions

Bookkeepers have more time to agree on the ordering of blocks, so there are fewer differences in opinion about block ordering. Later we will see how the network deals with conflicting blocks.

Once your transaction is bundled into a valid block, and that block is passed around the network, the transaction is "confirmed" with one confirmation. When the next block is added, your transaction is confirmed with two confirmations. There are situations where the newest blocks may be replaced by other blocks, kicking out transactions that look like they have already been confirmed.

There is a trade-off between the ease with which bookkeepers can agree on the ordering of transactions and the speed at which valid transactions are written into the blockchain. Having blocks once per day would make it easy to agree on ordering those blocks, but this is longer than people want to wait for their transactions to be confirmed.

Bitcoin blocks are created every ten minutes on average. Different cryptocurrencies have different block creation target times.

Problem: Who Can Create Blocks, and How Often?

Batching pending transactions into blocks that are propagated around the network makes sense. If there are discrepancies, they use the "longest chain rule" to decide which block wins.

Firstly, we need to manage the creation and frequency of blocks. If one party bundles all the blocks, we are back to a single, centralised control point, which we have set out to avoid.

Anyone needs to be able to create blocks and send them around the network. But how do we get a bunch of anonymous block-creators not to create blocks too quickly or slowly?

We can't trust block timestamps because these can be easily faked, and we also can't trust the individual bookkeepers who might accept their own blocks sooner than ten minutes.

Solution: Proof-of-Work

The solution is that all block-creators must play and win at a game of chance over the whole network, which takes some specific amount of time to play (ten minutes on average).

The game must not have a barrier to entry or shortcuts. The game needs an equal chance of winning, to have publicly displayable proof, and must not be cheatable.

The prize? Being allowed to create the next block.

Bitcoin uses something called "proof-of-work." Each block-creator bundles a bunch of transactions not yet been included in any blocks, then calculates a cryptographic hash from the block's data. The rule of Bitcoin's proof-of-work game of chance says that if the block's hash is smaller than a target number, then this block is considered a valid block that all bookkeepers should accept.

What if the hash of the block is bigger than this number? The block creator needs to alter the data going into the hash function and try hashing the block again. They could do this by adding or removing a transaction from the block, but that isn't the way to go about it.

In every Bitcoin block is a part of the block that can
be populated with an arbitrary number, changing the
number if the hash of the block doesn't meet the target
number. This number is called the "nonce" (number
once) and is separate from the financial transactions
in the block. Its only job is to change the input data for
the hash function.

Mining blocks

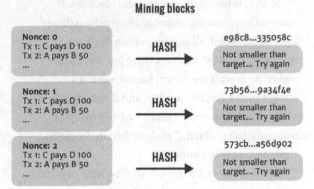

Each block creator puts together a block and fills the
nonce field with the number and hashes the block,
checks if the "hash is less than a target number" rule,
and gets to work on the next block if so. Otherwise,

they change the nonce (e.g., by adding one) and hash again and again. This process is known as mining.

This is elegantly described as a scratch-off puzzle in a paper by Miller et al. entitled "Nonoutsourceable Scratch-Off Puzzles to Discourage Bitcoin Mining Coalitions." Like scratch-off lottery cards, each miner must expend a bit of effort scratching off a puzzle to see if they have a winning ticket.

So the authority to create a valid block is self-assigned by repeating some tedious mathematical algorithms, which all computers can do. Note that mining is a tedious, repetitive job. Take some transactions with the nonce, hash it, see if it's smaller than a certain number, and if not, repeat with a different nonce. It is not "solving complex mathematical problems" as described in the media. Hashing is easy but boring.

Proof-of-work also avoids another kind of attack, a Sybil attack. A Sybil attack is when a network is overwhelmed by multiple forged identities all under the control of a single actor, like Facebook or Twitter bots.

In Bitcoin, your chance of winning a block is proportional to how much hashing power you control. Proof-of-work is computationally expensive in terms of electricity and hardware (i.e., cash), which means it is expensive to try to overwhelm the network with hashing power, which increases the attack costs to a bad actor. If you have all this hashing power available, you might as well put it to work finding blocks and making money (well, bitcoins) instead of trying to subvert the network, so the theory goes.

Problem: Incentivising Block Creators

But all of this tedious hashing needs resources: computers, electricity, bandwidth, and this costs money. How can we incentivise the block creators to create blocks and keep the system running?

Solution: Transaction Fees

The solution is to pay the block creators for their time and resources. But a third party paying them would defeat the purpose. US dollars or any fiat currency would not work either, as banks can be instructed to freeze bank accounts.

An internal or intrinsic incentivisation scheme avoids third-party control. This is implemented as a per transaction fee, so the block creator gets a commission from each transaction. Bitcoin's solution is based on people adding voluntary transaction fees, and the block creators prioritise transactions with higher fees over those with lower fees.

Incentivisation via voluntary transaction fees

A pays B 50 (fee for miner: 0.1)
C pays D 500 (fee for miner: 0.08)
E pays F 0.5 (fee for miner: 0.06)
A pays E 50 (fee for miner: 0.02)
E pays G 50 (fee for miner: 0.01)
G pays B 50 (fee for miner: 0)

> Build my block with highest fee transactions

Alice can optionally add a fee for the miner who mines her transaction. Fees tend to go up when many transactions are queuing up to get into blocks and down again in times with fewer transactions.

Problem: How to Bootstrap

How were block creators incentivised to keep creating blocks in the early days or now during slack periods when there may be periods where there are no transactions for some hours? The hashing work consumes electricity and costs miners money.

Solution: Block Rewards

The second and currently much larger incentive for block-creators to create blocks is the "block reward." The block creator can write a cheque to themselves once per block for up to a certain amount. Block rewards kick start the system, then are phased out gradually with transaction fees to replace them.

Bootstrapping the incentive scheme

```
Block                                         MINER'S REWARD
Coinbase Tx: Create 12.5 BTC for me  ◄──────
Tx 1: A pays B 50 (fee for miner: 0.1)
Tx 2: C pays D 500 (fee for miner: 0.08)
...
```

The first transaction in a block is called the coinbase transaction, the only way to create bitcoins. The block creator can create bitcoins up to a limit specified by the Bitcoin protocol. A limit of 50 BTC per block in 2009 and reduced by half every 210,000 blocks, which is about every four years. Currently (mid-2018) the maximum block reward is 12.5 BTC, with the next reduction to occur on block 630,000, estimated to occur in May 2020. These block rewards have created around 17 million bitcoins to date. The maximum number of bitcoins ever created (under current rules) will be a sliver under 21 million, which should be created a little before the year 2140.

They receive BTC in return for tediously hashing to create valid blocks. Block creators are not obligated to include any transactions in their blocks; they choose to because the transactions contain transaction fees.

The beauty of this system is that the payment for creating blocks comes from the protocol itself rather than an external third party.

Problem: More Hashing, Faster Blocks, More Monetary Supply

If anyone can create valid blocks and get paid for it, then surely, by throwing more computers at the hashing, they can create valid blocks quicker and get paid more. By doubling the amount of hashing power, they can, on average, double the speed at which they can create valid blocks.

But this, unchecked, would cause havoc. Throwing more hashing power (i.e., computers) at the block creation process would cause blocks to be created faster and faster. Remember, we want blocks to be created slowly so that the bookkeepers have a better chance of staying in consensus.

BTC would be created faster and faster, creating a huge supply and possibly decreasing the value of each unit.

Solution: Difficulty

The network needs to slow down if blocks are created quicker than one block every ten minutes. The answer lies in changing the target number for the hash calculation. Variations in this target number can make it easier or harder for the network to find hashes that fall below this number. Making the target number smaller slows down the rate at which valid blocks are created.

In Bitcoin, the target number is mathematically calculated from a number called the "difficulty." The difficulty changes every 2016 blocks (about two weeks). The faster the previous 2016 blocks were created, the more the difficulty increases. As difficulty increases, the target number becomes smaller, making it harder and slower to find valid blocks.

If more hashing or mining power is added, then blocks get created faster until the next difficulty change, slowing block creation down. If mining power leaves the network, blocks are made slower until the next time the difficulty change. And this is all done without a central coordinator.

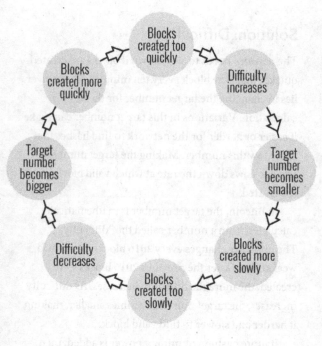

Problem: Block Ordering

Blocks are passed around the network slower than individual pending transactions. But how do you know what order the blocks should be? In a book, each page has a unique page number, and you know that the pages follow in ascending order. If the pages fall out, you can put the book back together again in the right order.

In principle, each block could get a unique "block number," yes. The miners start mining block 1,000. Someone might get to work mining block 1,000, so when someone else has found block 1,000, they can submit block 1,001 and claim the block reward. They can just hash an empty block 1,001 that refers to block 1,000 with a coinbase reward transaction and no other transactions.

What restricts miners to ensure they mine only the next block? How is "mining ahead" prevented?

Solution: A Block Chain

Instead of having each block have a "block number," each block refers to the previous block by its hash. Miners must include the previous block's hash in the block they create.

This means that to mine block 1,001, miners need to know the hash of block 1,000. Until 1,000 has been mined, 1,001 can't be mined. This forces miners to focus on block 1,000, and no miner can skip ahead. Thus, a chain of blocks is created, held together by block hashes.

A blockchain where each block includes the previous block's hash, rather than a sequential block number.

An additional benefit of blocks linking through their hashes is internal consistency. Let's say the latest block that has been passed around the network is block 1,000. If a rogue bookkeeper attempts to tamper with a previous block, say, block 990, and attempts to republish that block to other bookkeepers, they could:

1. Publish block 990 with new data but using the old hash

or

2. Publish block 990 with new data and a new valid hash (i.e., "re-mine" the block)

In the first case, the block will be considered invalid by all other bookkeepers because it is internally inconsistent (the block's hash doesn't match the data inside it), and in the second case, the hash of block 990 won't match the reference found in block 991. This is what is meant when blockchains are described as immutable. Of course, nothing is immutable (can't be changed), but blockchains are easy for others to tell if data has been modified.

Problem: Block Clashes / Consensus

If a bookkeeper receives two valid blocks from two different block creators at the same time, and they both reference the hash of the same previous block, how does the bookkeeper know which one to throw away? How does the network come to a *consensus* about which block to use? And if a miner receives two valid but competing blocks, how do they know which block to build the next block on?

Solution: Longest Chain Rule

There is another protocol rule called the longest chain rule. If a miner sees two valid blocks at the same block height, they can mine on either block (usually the first seen). Others will also make their decisions and eventually one of the blocks will have another block mined on it, then another, and another. The longest chain is considered the chain of record, and the discarded block is called an orphan.

The discarded transactions are never considered a part of a valid block and are "unconfirmed." They'll be included in later blocks along with other unconfirmed transactions, assuming they don't conflict with the transactions that have already been confirmed in the blockchain.

Problem: Double Spend

Although the longest chain rule seems sensible, it can be used to create mischief in a deliberate double spend. Here is how you could do it:

1. Create two transactions using the same bitcoins: one payment to an online retailer, the other to yourself (i.e., to another address you control).

2. Only broadcast the transaction that is the payment to the retailer.

3. When the payment gets added in an "honest" block, the retailer sees this and sends you goods.

4. Create a longer chain of blocks that excludes the payment to the retailer and replaces it with the payment to yourself.

5. Publish the longer chain. Bookkeepers will reorganize their blockchains, discarding the honest block containing the payment to the retailer and replacing it with the longer chain you published. The honest block is said to be "orphaned" and does not exist.

6. The original payment to the retailer will be deemed invalid by the honest nodes because those bitcoins have already been spent in your longer, substituted chain. You will have received your goods, but the network will reject the payment to the retailer.

1, 2, 3. "Pay the retailer" transaction is included in a block

4, 5. Attacker publishes a longer chain which includes the 'double spend'

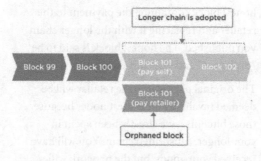

6. Original transaction (Pay the retailer) is no longer valid, as those coins were spent in Block 101 (pay self)

Solution: Wait About Six Blocks

Therefore, common advice for people receiving bitcoins is to wait for the transaction to be a few blocks deep (i.e., to have a few blocks mined on top of it). At this point the amount of mining that must be done to create a competing chain longer than the existing chain is enormous, so rational miners prefer to create legitimate blocks rather than trying to subvert the network.

If someone wants to replace blocks, they must create blocks quickly and overtake the rest of the network. If more than 50 percent of the network's total hash power is used to rewrite blocks, then it will be able to do so because it will create blocks faster than the other, less powerful half. This is called a 51 percent attack. Smaller amounts of hash power can also be used to rewrite the blockchain but with a lower probability of success. 51 percent attacks have been successfully performed on unpopular coins with few miners.

Which Coins?

With physical cash, each coin or banknote is a unique object. You can't pay *the same coin or banknote* to two people. However, digital money doesn't work that way. Your income goes into the bank's account and is immediately jumbled with all the other money

that is in there. When you make a payment, your total
balance is reduced. You cannot specify which dollar
you are spending. You just say, "Use eight dollars
from the pool of money that is my account balance."
This non-specificity promotes the fungibility of digital
money, that is, one dollar in an account is the same
as another.

Bitcoin is digital, but it works like physical cash.
With cash, you open your wallet, take a ten-dollar
note, pay eight dollars for your coffee, and expect
two dollars in change. For every Bitcoin payment you
make, you must specify exactly *which* specific coins
you are spending. In the same way that blocks build on
each other by referring to the previous block's hash,
transactions also refer to each other using a previous
transaction's hash. You say, "Take *this* bundle of
money from this transaction and pay some of it to *this*
account and return the change to me."

In a hypothetical transaction example, 1.427
bitcoins are removed from address 17tVxts…QM,
0.5999 bitcoins are sent to 1Ce2Qzz…wK, and 0.827
bitcoins are returned to 17tVxts…QM, plus a 0.0001
mining fee.

Hence all bitcoins are traceable. You can see
the exact composition of every lump of Bitcoin that

comes into your account—what it is composed of and where it came from—traceable to every previous account, back to when it was first created in a coin base transaction.

I say "lump of money" specifically, rather than "each Bitcoin" because you don't send bitcoins coin by coin; you send a total amount. Let's see how this works with an example.

Let's assume you are friends with a Bitcoin miner who created 12.5 BTC when they successfully mined a block. The 12.5 BTC is like a single banknote in a physical wallet and must be spent entirely. Since you have no bitcoins, they pity you and give you 1 BTC. So the miner creates a transaction spending that 12.5 BTC "lump" to two recipients: 1 BTC to you and 11.5 BTC back to herself. You now have a 1 BTC "lump" in your account.

You're lucky, and a few other people give you BTC, receiving "lumps" of 2 BTC and 3 BTC, totalling 6 BTC in your wallet, in three lumps: 1 BTC, 2 BTC, and 3 BTC.

If you want to give 1.5 BTC to another friend, you could do it in a few different ways:

Option 1: Spend the 2 BTC lump
You'd create a transaction that looks like this:
Spend: 2 BTC lump
Pay: 1.5 BTC to your friend, 0.5 BTC lump as change
back to yourself

Option 2: Spend the 3 BTC lump
You'd create a transaction that looks like this:
Spend: 3 BTC lump
Pay: 1.5 BTC to your friend, 1.5 BTC lump as change
back to yourself

Option 3: Spend the 1 BTC and 2 BTC lumps
You'd create a transaction that looks like this:
Spend: 1 BTC and 2 BTC lumps
Pay: 1.5 BTC to your friend, 1.5 BTC lump as change
back to yourself

Option 4: Spend the 1 BTC and 3 BTC lumps
You'd create a transaction that looks like this:
Spend: 1 BTC and 3 BTC lumps
Pay: 1.5 BTC to your friend, 2.5 BTC lump as change
back to yourself

Option 5: Spend the 1 BTC and 2 BTC and
3 BTC lumps
You'd create a transaction that looks like this:
Spend: 1 BTC and 2 BTC and 3 BTC lumps
Pay: 1.5 BTC to your friend, 4.5 BTC lump as change
back to yourself

These are all different transactions, but all achieve the same thing. The lumps of money in your account are called UTXOs, which stands for Unspent Transaction Outputs. Most people think in terms of "account balances" whereas Bitcoin "thinks" in transactions. Bitcoin would describe Option One as follows:

Option One: Spend the 2 BTC lump

Transaction inputs: (money being spent)

1.   2 BTC lump

Transaction outputs: (money not yet spent)

This whole transaction is hashed, giving it a Transaction ID, which future transactions can use.

You started with lumps of 1, 2, and 3 BTC. You spent the 2 BTC lump and got 0.5 BTC back. So you're left with three lumps: 1 BTC, 3 BTC, and the new 0.5 BTC lump. Anyone can trace the 0.5 BTC lump back to its original 2 BTC lump and then further trace it to the account which it came from originally.

Spending Unspent Transaction Outputs (UTxOs)

BEFORE

Address 1mk41QrLLeC9Cwph6UgV4GZ5nRfejQFsSUTxOs:

> 1 BTC from address 1Lna... eEM1
>
> 2 BTC from address 185f... s7f2
>
> 3 BTC from address 1Lna... eEM1

Transaction
Inputs (spend these):

> 2 BTC from address 185f...s7f2

Outputs (create these):

> 1.5 BTC to address 1gg2...94jc
>
> 0.5 BTC to address 1mk41...ejQFsS

NOTE:
If you wanted to include a miner fee, you'd reduce the "change" by the fee amount, e.g. from 0.5 to 0.495 BTC.

The sum of the outputs must be equal to or less than the sum of the inputs.

AFTER

Address 1mk41QrLLeC9Cwph6UgV4GZ5nRfejQFsSUTxOs:

> 1 BTC from address 1Lna... eEM1
>
> 0.5 BTC from address 185f... s7f2
>
> 3 BTC from address 1Lna... eEM1

What Next?

The transaction is created and signed using the sender's private keys. Then, it is then sent to a node (bookkeeper) who validates it according to business rules and technical rules, and if found valid, the bookkeeper puts it in a pool of "unconfirmed transactions," called a *mempool* or *memory pool*. Each bookkeeper follows the same process. Eventually a block creator may pack it into a block, and if so, start mining the block. If the miner successfully mines the block, they propagate the block to other miners and bookkeepers, and each node records this transaction as confirmed in a block.

Peer-to-Peer

When people say Bitcoin is "peer-to-peer," what do they mean?

First, *data* is sent between bookkeepers in a peer-to-peer way, i.e., directly and not via a central server. Transactions and blocks are sent between bookkeepers who are as important in status as each other—that is, they are peers. They use the internet to send data

instead of third-party infrastructure like the SWIFT
network used by major banks.

Second, Bitcoin *payments* are peer-to-peer (i.e.,
with no middleman). A *physical cash* transaction is
peer-to-peer, the payer and the recipient. Bitcoin also
has intermediaries such as miners and bookkeepers.
With Bitcoin payments, the intermediaries are *non-
specific* and can act in lieu of each other, whereas
traditional banks and centralised payment services
are *specific* intermediaries. You can't instruct another
bank other than yours to move your money, but
any miner can add your transaction to a block they
are mining.

Peer-to-peer models data distribution, where each
peer shares updates. Peer-to-peer is in many ways less
efficient than client-server, as data is replicated and
validated many times, once per machine. However,
the network can continue operating if some nodes
temporarily lose connectivity. And peer-to-peer
networks are more robust and resistant to shut down,
whether accidental or deliberate.

In anonymous and untrusted peer-to-peer
networks, you need to operate on the basis that anyone
could be a bad actor. So every peer needs to validate
transactions and blocks, rather than trusting other

peers. The network acts honestly if populated by many honest nodes. Next, we examine the limits of bad behaviour and the related costs and incentives.

Miscreants

What can and can't miscreants do?

The impact of a malicious *bookkeeper* is limited. They can withhold transactions and refuse to pass them to other bookkeepers, or they can present a false view of the state of the blockchain to anyone asking them. A quick check with other bookkeepers will reveal any discrepancies.

Malicious *miners* can cause a little more impact. They can:

- Attempt to create blocks that include or exclude specific transactions of their choosing.

- Create a double spend by attempting to create a "longer chain" of blocks that make previously accepted blocks become "orphans" and not part of the main chain.

But they can't:

- Steal bitcoins from your account.

- Create bitcoins out of thin air.

So the impact of a malicious miner is also limited. Furthermore, a miner discovered enabling double spends could quickly be cut off if the rest of the network informally agrees to act.

Summary

Transactions are payment instructions of specific amounts of Bitcoin (UTXOs) from one user-generated account (address) to another. The bookkeepers then add valid transactions to their *mempool* and distribute them to other bookkeepers they are connected to.

Miners gather these individual transactions into blocks and compete to mine their blocks by tweaking the block's nonce field until the block's hash is smaller than some target number. The target number is based on the difficulty setting at the time, which is derived from the time taken to mine the previous 2016 blocks to have one new mined block every ten minutes. Miners can receive created BTC and transaction fees which they may credit themselves.

The blocks link to each other by the Bitcoin blockchain, which is recorded almost simultaneously on thousands of computers worldwide.

There is no central authority who controls the ledger or who can censor specific transactions.

Different blockchain platforms or systems work differently. The solution may be simpler, as we will see later with private blockchains where censorship resistance is not a critical factor.

Bitcoin's Ecosystem

Putting this all together, we can see that the Bitcoin ecosystem consists of miners and bookkeepers focused on building and maintaining the blockchain. Exchanges and cryptocurrency payment processors bridge the fiat and crypto worlds.

Bitcoin in Practice

While the theory sounds good, Bitcoin in practice is not as decentralised as you might believe. By some metrics it is not performing as well as some proponents might lead you to believe.

Bookkeeping Nodes

While around ten thousand nodes perform bookkeeping tasks and relay transactions and blocks, they mostly run the same software written and controlled by a small number of people. They are known as the "Bitcoin Core" developers and the software is known as "Bitcoin Core."

The versions that are not Bitcoin Core all have slightly different rules but are not different enough to create incompatibilities. Some may have additional flags to signal that the bookkeepers would be prepared to adopt a rule change if needed.

Mining

Although anyone can mine, new hardware and chips are designed to be exceedingly efficient at performing the SHA-256 hashing. ASICs (Application Specific Integrated Chips) became the norm for mining in 2014 and outcompeted all other forms of hardware. Only a few entities can mine profitably, usually using special purpose "mining farms" clustered in areas of cheap electricity. The chart below shows miners and what proportion of blocks they have recently mined.

The proportion of blocks they have mined is roughly equivalent to their hashing power as a proportion of the network's total hashing power.

Some of these are single mining entities. Others are syndicates that anyone can join, contribute hash power, and receive rewards in proportion to their contributions. Around 80 percent of the hash power is estimated to be controlled by BTC.com, Antpool, BTC.TOP, F2Pool, and viaBTC. All are Chinese groups, and a company called Bitmain owns BTC.com and Antpool. Hence, if only the top three mining pools collaborate, they can reorganise blocks and arrange double spends, and no one could stop them as they represent more than 50 percent of the total hashing power.

It is often argued that miners wouldn't do this because it would cause a loss of confidence in Bitcoin and thus cause the price to fall, and their Bitcoin stock would be worth less. However, an enterprising group of miners who carried this out could build a temporary large short trading position just before executing a double spend and profit on the fall in price of BTC.

Mining Hardware

As discussed, miners use special purpose chips called
ASICs designed and built to be efficient at SHA256
hashing. Commercial chip manufacturers have been
slow to design chips that are specifically built to be
efficient at SHA256 hashing, so demand has created an
alternative specialised industry for supplying Bitcoin
ASICs. It has been estimated that Bitmain produces
hardware that mines 70–80 percent of the total blocks
in Bitcoin. Bitcoin hardware manufacturing is not
well decentralised.

BTC Ownership

Almost 90 percent of value is owned by fewer than 0.7
percent of the addresses. Of course, some large wallets
are controlled by exchanges that take custody of coins
on behalf of many users. Against that, some people
might spread their bitcoins across a large number of
wallets to not attract attention.

Upgrades to the Bitcoin Protocol

Upgrades to the Bitcoin network and protocols are also fairly centralised. Changes are suggested in "Bitcoin Improvement Proposals" (BIPs). These are documents that anyone may write, but they all end up on a single website: github.com/bitcoin/bips. If it gets written into the Bitcoin Core software on GitHub (github.com/bitcoin/Bitcoin), it forms the next version of "Bitcoin Core," the most used software. As we have seen, this is run by most participants.

Transaction Fees

TRANSACTION FEES ARE MEANT TO REPLACE BLOCK REWARDS

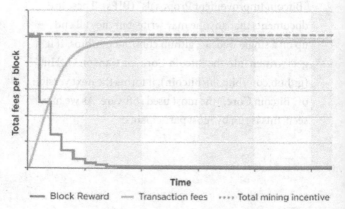

Time

— Block Reward · — · — Transaction fees · · · · Total mining incentive

In theory, the transaction fees collected per block are meant to compensate for the decrease in block reward as the network gets more popular. The reality is that this isn't working out.

Except for a brief spike at the end of 2017, the total transaction fees have stayed stubbornly low at approximately two hundred BTC per week. Compare this with the new 12,600 BTC generated from weekly coin base rewards. Without a significant increase in transaction fees to compensate, the economics of Bitcoin mining will change.

Bitcoin's Predecessors

Bitcoin, like most innovations, was not created in a vacuum. Bitcoin was built by drawing from previous experiences and piecing together various tried-and-tested concepts in an innovative way to come up with new characteristics for decentralised digital cash.

Below are some technologies and ideas that may have directly or indirectly inspired Bitcoin.

Digicash

David Chaum greatly impacted the movement toward a privacy-preserving digital asset that could settle financial obligations. Chaum described this concept in 1983 in a paper entitled "Blind Signatures for Untraceable Payments" in the journal *Advances in Cryptology Proceedings*. He wanted the customers to spend digital cash "lumps" at shops, who would then redeem the digital cash with the bank. The bank would see that the digital cash was good, but it did not know which of its customers the digital cash had originated from. Therefore, anonymous as far as the bank was concerned. Digicash was an Amsterdam-based company incorporated to commercialise this technology. The system was called eCash, sometimes *Chaumian* eCash, with the tokens themselves called CyberBucks. Although a few banks did some trials with CyberBucks, Digitcash filed for bankruptcy in 1998, unable to secure a deal to keep it afloat.

b-money

In November 1998, Wei Dai, an American-educated cryptography researcher and cypherpunk, published a short paper describing b-money under two protocols. b-money would operate on an untraceable network where senders and receivers would be identified only by digital pseudonyms (i.e., public keys). Transactions would be broadcast to a network of servers that would keep track of account balances and update them when they received signed transaction messages. Money creation would be agreed by the participants in a periodic auction.

Hashcash

In 1992, Cynthia Dwork and Moni Naor described
a technique for reducing junk emails in their paper
"Pricing via Processing or Combatting Junk Mail"
by creating a hoop that email senders would have to
jump through before sending emails. Email senders
would attach a kind of *proof* that they had incurred a
small "cost." Recipients would reject inbound emails
without these receipts. The "costs" would add up and
discourage spammers who send out millions of emails.
The "cost" wasn't a payment to a third party, but it
would be incurred as "work" in the form of repeated
calculations that had to be made to ensure an email
would be accepted. So the receipt would be a "proof"
that repeated calculations or "work" had been done,
leading to the phrase "proof-of-work."

In 1997, Adam Back proposed a similar idea and
described a "partial hash collision-based postage
scheme," which he named "Hashcash." He followed up
in 2002 with a paper, "Hashcash—A Denial of Service
Counter-Measure," describing improvements and
applications of proof-of-work, including hashcash as a
minting mechanism for Wei Dai's b-money electronic
cash proposal.

E-gold

E-gold was a website opened in 1996 operated by Gold
& Silver Reserve Inc. (G&SR) under the name "e-gold
Ltd," allowing customers to open accounts and trade
units of gold between each other. The digital units
were backed by gold stored in a bank safe deposit
box in Florida, USA. E-gold didn't ask users to prove
their identity. It was reported to have up to 3.5 million
accounts in 165 countries in 2005, with a thousand
new accounts opening every day, but the website was
eventually shut down due to fraud and allegations
of facilitation of crime. Unlike Bitcoin, it had a
centralised ledger.

Liberty Reserve

Liberty Reserve, based in Costa Rica, allowed
customers to open accounts with nothing more than
a name, email address, and birth date. Liberty Reserve
made no attempts to verify these. As a result of its
relaxed controls, Liberty Reserve was used extensively
for criminal proceeds: more than six billion dollars
of it, according to ABC News. It served over a million

customers before it was shut down in 2013 by the US government under the Patriot Act.

Napster

Napster was a peer-to-peer file-sharing system that was live between 1999 and 2001. It was created by Shawn Fanning and Sean Parker and was popular with people who liked to share music and didn't like to pay for it. The idea was to allow anyone to copy and share content saved on users' hard drives. At its peak, the service had about eighty million registered users. It was eventually shut down because of its relaxed approach to sharing copyrighted material.

Napster's technical weakness was that it had central servers. User's machines would send the search request to Napster's central servers, which would return a list of computers storing that song and allow the user to connect to one of them to download the song. Although Napster didn't host the material, it made it easy for users to discover others who did. Centralised services and entities running those services are easy to shut down, so its role was replaced by BitTorrent, a decentralised peer-to-peer file-sharing system.

Mojo Nation

According to CEO Jim McCoy, Mojo Nation was an open-source project that was a cross between Napster and eBay. Launched in or around 2000, it combined file sharing with microtransactions of a token called Mojo, so file-sharers could be compensated for sharing content. Mojo Nation failed to gain traction, but Zooko Wilcox-O'Hearn, who worked on Mojo Nation, later founded Zcash, a cryptocurrency focused on transaction privacy.

BitTorrent

BitTorrent is a successful peer-to-peer file-sharing protocol still widely used today. It was developed by BitTorrent Inc., a company cofounded by Bram Cohen, who worked on Mojo Nation. BitTorrent is popular with those sharing music and movies, users who may once have used Napster. Each search request is made from user to user rather than via a central search server, so it is hard to censor and shut down.

Whether we consider money (e-Gold, Liberty Reserve, Bitcoin, etc.), or data (Napster, BitTorrent, etc.), the evidence shows that decentralised protocols are more resilient to being shut down. Decentralisation is driven by concerns that authorities are overextending their reach into private social matters.

Bitcoin's Early History

Some Bitcoin proponents say "Bitcoin (the protocol) has never been hacked," but they are wrong. Bitcoin has been hacked. Here is a selection of events from historyofbitcoin.org and the Bitcoin Wiki with my comments about these events.

2007

A pseudonymous Satoshi Nakamoto began working on Bitcoin.

18 Aug 2008

The website bitcoin.org was registered using anonymousspeech.com, a broker that registers domains on behalf of customers who can choose to remain anonymous.

31 Oct 2008

The Bitcoin whitepaper, written under the pseudonym
Satoshi Nakamoto, was released on the mailing list
metzdowd.com, loved by cypherpunks. Wikipedia has
this to say about cypherpunks:

> A cypherpunk is any activist advocating
> widespread use of strong cryptography and
> privacy-enhancing technologies as a route
> to social and political change. Originally
> communicating through the cypherpunks
> electronic mailing list, informal groups aimed to
> achieve privacy and security through proactive
> use of cryptography.

This short whitepaper is regarded by Bitcoin believers
as a sort of bible.

3 Jan 2009

The first block was mined. At that moment, the first
bitcoins were created out of thin air and recorded on
Bitcoin's blockchain in the first block—block zero.
The transaction that contains the mining reward, the
"coinbase" transaction, contains the text:

> The Times 03/Jan/2009 Chancellor on brink of
> second bailout for banks.

The text refers to a headline of the UK newspaper *The Times*. This is regarded as proof that the block cannot have been mined significantly earlier than that date, and the headline was presumably chosen deliberately for its implication: When banks fail, their losses are socialized; here is Bitcoin—it doesn't need banks.

An interesting aside: The fifty BTC mined in the first block are not spendable. They sit in address 1A1zP1eP5QGefi2DMPTfTL5SLmv7DivfNa, but the account holder, presumably Satoshi, whoever he, she, or they may be, cannot transfer them to anyone else due to some quirk in the code.

9 Jan 2009

Version 0.1 of the Bitcoin software was released by Satoshi Nakamoto, along with its source code. This allowed people to review the code and download and run the software, becoming bookkeepers and miners. Developers could scrutinise the code and build on it if they wanted to contribute.

12 Jan 2009

The first Bitcoin payment was made from Satoshi's address to Hal Finney's address in block 170, the

first recorded movement of bitcoins. Hal Finney
was a cryptographer, cypherpunk, and coder,
and some people believe he was partly behind the
Satoshi pseudonym.

6 Feb 2010

The first Bitcoin exchange, "The Bitcoin Market," was
created by bitcointalk.org forum user "dwdollar."

Update

I am trying to create a market where Bitcoins are
treated as a commodity. People will be able to trade
Bitcoins for dollars and speculate on the value. In
theory, this will establish a real-time exchange rate
so we will all have a clue what the current value of
a bitcoin is, compared to a dollar. I have an early
version up at http://98.168.168.27:8080/.

This is only a small demonstration of what I have in
mind and to show everyone I'm actively working
on it. Feel free to register and try it out. You will get
10 phoney dollars and 10,000 phoney bitcoins to
trade. Only the limited orders work. Market orders
will come later.

Previously, people traded bitcoins in a relatively
unstructured way in chat rooms and message boards.

An exchange is the first step toward making it easier for people to buy or sell bitcoins and increasing price transparency.

22 May 2010

Pizza day! This was the first documented time bitcoins were used to pay for something in the real world. Laszlo Hanyecz, a programmer in Florida, USA, offered to pay 10,000 BTC for a pizza on the bitcointalk forum.

Pizza for bitcoins?

I'll pay 10,000 bitcoins for a couple of pizzas...like maybe 2 large ones so I have some left over for the next day. I like having left over pizza to nibble on later. You can make the pizza yourself and bring it to my house or order it for me from a delivery place, but what I'm aiming for is getting food delivered in exchange for bitcoins where I don't have to order or prepare it myself, kind of like ordering a 'breakfast platter' at a hotel or something, they just bring you something to eat and you're happy!

I like things like onions, peppers, sausage, mushrooms, tomatoes, pepperoni, etc. just standard stuff no weird fish topping or anything like that. I also like regular cheese pizzas which may be cheaper to prepare or otherwise acquire.

If you're interested, please let me know and we can work out a deal.

Thanks,
Laszlo

Another developer, Jeremy Sturdivant ("jercos"), took up the offer and called Domino's Pizza (not Papa Johns as frequently reported) and had two pizzas delivered to Laszlo. He received 10,000 BTC from Laszlo.

Re: Pizza for bitcoins?

I just want to report that I successfully traded 10,000 bitcoins for pizza.

Pictures: http://heliacal.net/~solar/bitcoin/pizza/

Thanks jercos!

Laszlo kept the offer open and, over the next month, received several pizzas for 10,000 BTC each time before cancelling the offer:

> **Re: Pizza for bitcoins?**
>
> Well I didn't expect this to be so popular but I can't really afford to keep doing it since I can't generate thousands of coins a day anymore. Thanks to everyone who bought me pizza already but I'm kind of holding off on doing any more of these for now.

This is the first transaction where bitcoins were used for economic activity other than a straight buy or sell.

17 Jul 2010

Jed McCaleb converted his card-trading exchange into a Bitcoin-trading exchange. "Mt Gox," usually pronounced "mount gox," stands for "Magic: The Gathering Online eXchange." Magic: The Gathering is a collectable card game, and the website was initially used to trade cards. Initially, you could fund your Mt Gox account using PayPal, but in October, they switched to Liberty Reserve. Mt Gox would eventually collapse in November 2013–February 2014, but in its heyday, it was the largest and most well-known and well-used exchange.

15 Aug 2010

Bitcoin's protocol got hacked. A potential vulnerability was discovered, and someone exploited this vulnerability in block 74,638 to create 184 billion bitcoins for themselves. This strange transaction was quickly discovered, and, with the consent of the majority of the community, the whole blockchain was "forked," reverting it to a previous state (we will discuss forks later).

So much for the immutability of Bitcoin's blockchain: there are always exceptions.

The bug was fixed. Bruno Skvorc has written a good explanation of how it happened on his blog bitfalls.com, and the bitcointalk forum has a thread where key developers discussed the bug.

18 Sep 2010

The first mining pool, Slush's pool, mined its first block. A mining pool is an organisation where participants combine their hash power for a better chance of winning a block. The participants split the rewards in proportion to their hash power contributions, like a lottery syndicate. Mining pools have grown in significance over time.

7 Jan 2011

Twelve BTC were exchanged for $300,000,000,000,000. This is probably the highest exchange rate Bitcoin has ever achieved. The dollars in question, however, were Zimbabwean dollars. The Zimbabwean dollar is a good example of what can go wrong in a failing economy and a reminder that fiat currencies need to be well managed.

9 Feb 2011

On the Mt Gox Bitcoin exchange, Bitcoin reached parity with the US dollar (one BTC = one USD).

6 Mar 2011

Jed McCaleb sold the Mt Gox website and exchange to a French entrepreneur Mark Karpeles, on the premise that Mark would do a better job expanding it. Mark did not live up to these hopes. Mt Gox filed for bankruptcy in 2014, and Mark eventually landed in jail.

27 Apr 2011

VirWoX, a website that allowed customers to convert
between fiat currencies and Linden dollars (the
virtual currency for the computer game Second
Life), integrated Bitcoin. People could now exchange
directly between bitcoins and Linden dollars. This
was possibly the first virtual currency to virtual
currency exchange.

1 Jun 2011

WIRED magazine published a famous article,
"Underground Website Lets You Buy Any Drug
Imaginable," by Adrian Chen. It described a
website called the Silk Road, launched in February
2011 and run by Ross William Ulbricht under the
nickname "Dread Pirate Roberts." The Silk Road was
described as an "eBay for drugs"—only accessible
through the special browser Tor, which matched
buyers and sellers of drugs and other illegal or
questionable paraphernalia. Bitcoins were used as the
payment mechanism.

The article describes Bitcoin:

As for transactions, Silk Road doesn't accept credit cards, PayPal or any other form of payment that can be traced or blocked. The only money good here is Bitcoins.

Bitcoins have been called a "cryptocurrency," the online equivalent of a brown paper bag of cash... They are purportedly untraceable and have been championed by cyberpunks, libertarians and anarchists...

To purchase something on Silk Road, you need first to buy some bitcoins... Then, create an account on Silk Road, deposit some bitcoins, and start buying drugs. One Bitcoin is worth about $8.67, though the exchange rate fluctuates wildly every day.

This was the first time Bitcoin came to the attention of a wide audience. The Silk Road was eventually taken down by US authorities in October 2013, though many copycats have taken its place.

14 Jun 2011

Wikileaks and other organisations began to accept bitcoins for donations. While it is relatively easy for a government to lean on traditional payment systems (banks, PayPal, etc.) to monitor transactions, block assets, and freeze accounts, cryptocurrencies provide an alternative funding mechanism. Whether this is good or bad, of course, is a matter of opinion.

20 Jun 2011

Possibly the first documented evidence of a physical brick-and-mortar merchant accepting Bitcoin as a means of payment. Room 77, a restaurant based in Berlin, Germany, sold fast food for bitcoins.

Restaurant/Pub in Berlin accepts Bitcoin as a means of payment

I was in Berlin-Kreuzberg today and I came across the room77, the Bitcoin accepted as a means of payment.

For not even a BTC a full dinner, which consisted of a coke and a delicious monster cheeseburger. ☺ Possibly the first restaurant in Germany that officially accepts bitcoin?

It is always worthwhile for this sensational exchange rate. ☺

2 Sep 2011

Mike Caldwell started creating physical bitcoins, which he called Casascius coins. They are physical discs of metal, each with a unique private key embedded behind a hologram sticker. Each coin's private key is linked to an address funded with a specified number of bitcoins, as is depicted on the coin.

These Casascius coins are the physical representations used in many stock photos in media articles about bitcoins. They are also prized as collector's items and cost more than the value of the bitcoins contained in them, especially the first edition, which had a spelling mistake.

8 May 2012

Satoshi Dice was a gambling website launched on April 24, 2012. Users could send bitcoins to specific addresses with a chance of winning up to 64,000 times their original stake. On May 8, it became responsible for over half the transaction volume on the Bitcoin blockchain. Early adopters seemed to have a penchant for gambling, and there wasn't much else they could do with their bitcoins.

Unlike other online casinos where users have to trust that the house is not cheating, Satoshi Dice was provably fair, using deterministic cryptographic hashes as the random number generators. Of course, the house had an edge, but the edge was small, known (1.9 percent), and was demonstrably adhered to.

This development started the debate about what "spamming" a network with transactions means when there are no terms of service. It also started the community thinking about what fair transaction fees should be.

28 Nov 2012

Bitcoin's first block reward halving day: On block 210,000, the reward halved from fifty BTC to twenty-five BTC, slowing the rate of generation of bitcoins. Transaction fees then were insignificant, so this halving day reduced by half each block's financial reward for miners.

2 May 2013

The first of many two-way Bitcoin ATMs was launched in San Diego, California. This was a machine where you could buy bitcoins or sell your bitcoins for cash. Many were found to be unprofitable, as demand didn't meet expectations.

Jul 2013

The first Bitcoin ETF (Exchange Traded Fund) proposal was filed with the United States Securities and Exchange Commission. An ETF could make an investment in Bitcoin more accessible to the public.

6 Aug 2013

Bitcoin was classified as a currency by a judge in Texas, USA. This was one of many arguments and determinations of what Bitcoin is: Currency? Property? A new thing? There may never be a globally consistent definition.

Bitcoin's categorisation has tax and other implications that differ by jurisdiction. The classification of bitcoins and cryptocurrencies may mean the difference between zero or punitive tax rates in any given tax regime (see below, 20 Aug 2013).

9 Aug 2013

Bitcoin's price became searchable through Bloomberg software, which is popular with traders in traditional financial markets. "XBT" was chosen to represent Bitcoin, consistent with ISO currency code standards. ISO currency codes (e.g., USD, GBP, etc.) first two letters denote the country and the third letter denotes the currency unit. The symbol "BTC," if adopted, would indicate a currency of Bhutan. Precious metals such as gold (XAU) and silver (XAG) are also considered a "currency" but start with X as they are not associated with a country. Bitcoin follows the currency standard for precious metals.

20 Aug 2013

Bitcoins were ruled as private money in Germany, with tax exemptions if held for more than a year. If you bought a Bitcoin at a hundred dollars, then, after its price had risen to a thousand dollars, you exchanged it for Ether, another cryptocurrency, then you would have to record that as a capital gain of nine hundred

dollars and pay tax on that capital gain, even though
your assets were still in cryptocurrency and you
hadn't realised that gain in USD. So, depending on the
jurisdiction, tax authorities may consider the exchange
of cryptocurrencies as selling and buying with fiat
currency and want to see those transactions taxed.

22 Nov 2013

Richard Branson, the owner of Virgin Galactic,
announced he would accept bitcoins as payment for a
flight to space. Bitcoins and space travel—what a great
time to be alive!

28 Feb 2014

After a long saga of hacks, poor management practices,
lost coins, failed banking transactions, and other
incompetence, Mt Gox filed for bankruptcy protection
in Japan in February 2014. There are numerous
theories about what happened, the most compelling
being a combination of hackers draining the Mt Gox
hot wallets and management incompetence. The
story of Mt Gox deserves a book, but for a summary
it is worth reading the Wikipedia entry about this
sorry story.

After Mt Gox's implosion, Bitfinex became the world's largest exchange for a while.

Creditors to the bankrupt estate have not yet been compensated, and if they ever are, it will be in Japanese yen at a rate that roughly equates to four hundred dollars per Bitcoin—less than a tenth of Bitcoin's value at the time of writing.

Chapter 2

STORING AND SPENDING BITCOIN

Bitcoin's Price

Like gold or any other asset, bitcoins can be priced
in USD or any other currency. This means people
are willing to exchange BTC with USD, usually using
cryptocurrency exchanges. You can also buy and
sell bitcoins with anyone in the world, physically on
the street or over the internet, or using brokers who
mediate between buyers and sellers or trade on their
behalf. To trade BTC, you need to send or receive
BTC and receive or send the other asset, usually a
local currency.

   Like any other market-traded asset, the price of
Bitcoin fluctuates with supply and demand. At any
point in time, people trade at prices that they are
comfortable buying or selling at. If there is demand,
prices will increase. If more people want to sell
bitcoins, the price of bitcoins will drop. Later we will
go into more detail about how cryptocurrencies and
tokens can be priced, but here we will look specifically
at Bitcoin's price.

Bitcoin's Price History

Bitcoin's price has been a wild ride. A price rise to almost US $20,000 per Bitcoin and subsequent fall to the $6,000 levels caught the media's attention in 2018: that's a 60 percent crash.

Bitcoin appears cyclically volatile, with each cycle as dizzy as the previous.

The 2013–14 bubble peaked at $1,200 per Bitcoin, followed by an 80 percent crash.

The peak price on Mt Gox was almost $1,200 per Bitcoin, and then crashed to below $200, then traded lower to the $200–$300 range during the "Bitcoin winter" of 2014. These were painful times for holders of Bitcoin. There are different theories for the cause of this bubble—trading bot programs that automatically buy and sell and that you couldn't withdraw fiat from Mt Gox, only bitcoins. The Chinese government then announced that they would ban Bitcoin trading, and the price crashed.

But this was not the first bubble. In April 2013, the price rose from $15 to a peak of $266 before crashing to around $50 for another 80 percent crash.

A common theory was that people in Cyprus were buying bitcoins. Cyprus was in financial chaos.

Bank accounts were frozen, some ATMs were empty, and one-off taxes were applied to large bank account balances.

This bubble may seem quaint, but an 80 percent drop is an 80 percent drop, as stressful as it would be today.

Further back, we had the June 2011 bubble, where prices rose to $31 per Bitcoin, followed by an 80 percent crash.

Articles published in tech-focused magazines *WIRED* and *Gawker* helped to generate interest in Bitcoin, pushing the price from about $3 to a high of about $31. Over the next six months, the price slowly fell to below $5, more than 80 percent.

During the first bubble in July 2010, the cost rose to $0.09 per Bitcoin and ended with a 40 percent crash.

Interest grew about a new version of the Bitcoin software from an article published in a popular technical magazine, *Slashdot*. Pushing the price on the Bitcoin market up from less than one cent per Bitcoin to almost ten cents, the price fell 40 percent and traded sideways at about six cents per Bitcoin for a few months before increasing again.

Storing Bitcoins

You may hear that bitcoins are stored in wallets. If this were true, if you copied your wallet, you'd own double the number of bitcoins. It sadly does not work this way.

Ownership of bitcoins is recorded on Bitcoin's blockchain. So you can look at the blockchain and see that, at this time, a specific address has several bitcoins associated with it. For example, the address 1Jco97X5FbCkev7ksVDpRtjNNi4zX6Wy4r had 0.5 BTC sent to it, and that 0.5 BTC has not yet been sent elsewhere. Bitcoin's blockchain doesn't store balances of accounts; it stores transactions. The current balance of any account is the sum of all inbound and outbound transactions through that account.

Bitcoin wallets store private keys, and their software makes it easy for the user of the wallet to see how many coins they control and to make payments. If you cloned your wallet, you would be cloning your private keys, not doubling your bitcoins.

Software Wallet

Bitcoin wallets are apps that can at least:

- Create new Bitcoin addresses and store the corresponding private keys

- Display your addresses to someone who wants to send you a payment

- Display how many bitcoins are in your addresses

- Make Bitcoin payments

Let's explore each of these capabilities.

Address Creation

Creating new Bitcoin addresses is an offline operation and involves creating a public and private key pair. You can do this, if you like, using dice. This is different from any other account creation process where you ask a third party to create an account for you, for example, asking your bank or Facebook to assign you an account.

- Step 1: Generate some randomness and use it to pick a number from 1 to $2^{256}-1$. This is your private key.

- Step 2: Do some maths on it to generate a public key.

- Step 3: Hash your public key twice to create your Bitcoin address.

- Step 4: Save the private key and its corresponding address.

You assign yourself an address without checking if it has already been taken. What if someone else has already chosen your private key? The short answer is that this is extremely unlikely. 2^{256} is a big number, seventy-eight digits long, and you can pick any number up to that. Your chance of winning the UK lottery is 1 in 13,983,816, which only has eight digits. In practice, however, weaknesses can exist, and they rely on exploiting flaws in the random number generation for the private keys. If there is a flaw in the randomness when generating your private key, this flaw could be exploited to reduce the search space for a thief.

Address Display

When someone wants to send you bitcoins, you need to tell them your address—like telling someone your bank account number so they can send you money. There are a few ways to do this. One popular way is by showing it as a QR code.

Example Bitcoin address:
1LfSBaySpe6UBw4NoH9VLSGmnPvujmhFXV
Equivalent QR code:

QR codes are not magic. They are text encoded visually, making it easy for QR code scanners to read the code and convert it back into text.

Another way is to copy and paste the address:

> Please send me 1.5 BTC

Sure, what's your bitcoin address?

> It's 1MKe24pNsLmFYk9mJd1dXHkKj9h5YhoEey

Ok, sent

> Thanks, I see it now

Account Balance

The wallet needs to access an up-to-date version of the blockchain to know all the transactions involving its addresses. The wallet software can do this by storing the entire blockchain (known as a full node wallet) or connecting to a node elsewhere (lightweight wallet).

A full node wallet would contain over a hundred gigabytes of data and must be constantly connected over the internet to other Bitcoin nodes. So in many cases, this is not practical, and the wallet software connects to a server that hosts the blockchain.

Bitcoin Payments

The wallet also needs to make payments. To make a Bitcoin payment, the wallet generates a "transaction," which includes references to the coins that will be spent and the accounts where the coins will be sent. This transaction is then digitally signed using the private keys of the addresses holding the coins. Then, the transaction is sent to neighbouring nodes. The transactions eventually find their way to miners who add them to blocks.

Other Features

Good wallet software can back up private keys
(encrypted with a passphrase), generate one-time use
addresses for privacy, and hold addresses and private
keys for multiple cryptocurrencies.

Often wallets will allow you to split keys or set
up addresses requiring multiple digital signatures to
spend from.

You can split a private key into several parts so that
several parts are needed to create the original private
key, known as "sharding" or "splitting" a private
key. A common example is two-of-three sharding,
where a private key is split into three parts, any two
of which can be combined into the original key.
Similarly, you can have two-of-four, three-of-four, or
any combination of parts and total shards, generically
m-of-n. One algorithm to do this is using Shamir's
secret sharing. This lets you split a key and store parts
of it separately in different places, and if you lose one
or more pieces, it may not be catastrophic.

You can also create addresses that require multiple
digital signatures to make payments from them. These
are known as "multi-sig" addresses. Again, you can
have one-of-three, two-of-three, three-of-three, or

generically m-of-n. This has slightly better security properties than sharding a single private key. This lets you create a transaction, sign it, send it over the internet in the clear, and let someone else sign it before it is considered a valid transaction (key-splitting only results in one signature). These addresses let you create systems where multiple people need to sign or approve a transaction.

Software Wallet Examples

Examples of popular Bitcoin software wallets:

- Blockchain.info

- Electrum

- Jaxx

- Breadwallet

Note that I do not endorse these, and others are available. They could have bugs, backdoors, or vulnerabilities, and you must do your research before picking a wallet to use.

Hardware Wallets

Sometimes Bitcoin wallets can have a hardware component. Private keys are stored in chips on small handheld devices. Two popular hardware wallets are called "Trezor" and "Ledger Nano," but there are others.

These devices are specifically designed to store private keys securely and only respond to certain pre-programmed requests—"Please sign this transaction," and not "Show me the private key you are storing." Therefore, it is much harder for hackers to access these private keys.

The user interface software is run on an online machine. When signing the transaction, the unsigned transaction is sent to the hardware wallet, which returns the signed transaction without revealing the private key.

Hardware wallets are more secure than software-only wallets, but nothing is infallible.

Cold Storage

Remember, you don't store bitcoins; you store private keys. "Cold storage" is keeping a note of those private keys on a piece of paper or a computer not connected to the internet. Private keys are strings of characters like:

```
'KyVR7Y8xManWXf5hBj9s1iFD56E8d-
s2Em71vxvN73zhT99ANYCxf'
```

There are many ways of storing them. You can even engrave them on a ring that you wear, like Charlie Shrem did, according to *WIRED* magazine. You could store them on an offline computer that does not have a modem or network card or write them down and put them in a bank's locked deposit box.

One way of increasing security is to first encrypt the private key with a passphrase that you can remember and then store or print out the encrypted result. This means that even if someone gets hold of the device or printout, they'd need your passphrase before the private key is revealed. You can split keys or use multi-sig addresses for further security. This means if a thief finds one part, it is useless without another part, and if one part is lost, the other two will still work.

Hot Wallets

A hot wallet is a wallet that can sign and broadcast transactions without manual intervention. Exchanges need to manage many Bitcoin payments, as we will see later. Customers of exchanges like to withdraw bitcoins by clicking a button, causing an automated process to run and sign a Bitcoin transaction, moving bitcoins to the user's wallet. There is a trade-off between security and convenience. Online machines are easier to hack than offline machines. Exchanges keep only a small fraction of BTC in hot wallets, enough to satisfy customer demand.

Buying and Selling Bitcoins

You can buy bitcoins from anyone who has them. Likewise, you can sell bitcoins to anyone who wants them. Fortunately, there are various places where you are likely to find a group of people willing to trade at competitive prices—exchanges.

Exchanges

Like a stock exchange, a cryptocurrency exchange is a place (usually a website) that allows people to buy and sell between themselves, not directly with the exchange. People go to the exchange because they know they will likely get the best prices there.

The exchange also acts as the central clearing counterparty. All matched trades appear to be against the exchange rather than between the customers directly, providing anonymity for customers. Finally, the exchange controls customers' fiat money in its bank account and cryptocurrencies in its wallet.

How Do Cryptocurrency Exchanges Work?

Exchanges are based in different countries and support fiat currencies and cryptocurrencies. They all work roughly the same way using the same four steps:

1. Create account
2. Deposit
3. Trade
4. Withdraw

Create Account

To use an exchange, you need to open an account.
Exchanges are under regulatory scrutiny due to
the large amounts of money they process. The top
cryptocurrency exchanges match billions of dollars
of daily buys and sells. Most legitimate exchanges
have new customers submit details and evidence of
their identity, for example, passport and utility bills.
The documentation needed is proportional to the
value of fiat or cryptocurrencies you plan to transact.
Exchanges are now big business and take these
processes seriously.

Once the exchange is satisfied, your account is
created. Then you can log in and the next step is
to deposit.

Deposit

To buy or sell anything on an exchange, you need to
fund your account. This is like funding an account
with a traditional broker before being allowed to buy
traditional financial assets.

Exchanges have bank accounts and cryptocurrency
wallets. To fund your account, click on "Deposit,"
then follow the instructions. If you are funding

your account with fiat currency (presumably to buy cryptocurrency), the exchange will display a bank account for you to make a fiat currency transfer to. If you are funding your account with cryptocurrency (presumably to sell for fiat currency or trade for a different cryptocurrency), the exchange will display a cryptocurrency address for you to make a cryptocurrency transfer to.

Once the exchange has detected the transfer to their bank account or cryptocurrency address, the balance will be reflected in your "account balance" on the exchange's website, and you are ready to trade.

Trade

Prices are expressed in pairs: BTC/USD or BTCUSD with a number such as eight thousand. The way to read this is, "One unit of BTC costs eight thousand USD." Not all currencies can be traded for each other—it is up to the exchange as to which pairs they enable.

You will see a screen showing the prices at which people are willing to trade, and how much they are willing to trade at that price. You can decide either to match their prices, which will result in a matched trade, or submit orders that will rest in the order book until someone matches your price (if they ever do).

The larger amounts you want to buy or sell, the worse the prices. This is confusing for some people initially but is easily explained. The exchange will match you off with the person selling it at the cheapest price. Then, the person with the next best price, which will be slightly higher. Selling uses the same logic: the exchange will match you with the person willing to pay the highest price for it. Then, you will have to go to the next highest price, which will be slightly lower.

Withdraw

To withdraw fiat or cryptocurrency, you must instruct the exchange where you want it to go. When withdrawing fiat, the exchange needs your bank account details. Similarly, you need to tell the exchange your cryptocurrency address.

How Do Exchanges Make Money?

Exchanges make money by charging fees. Some charge withdrawal fees. Others charge by taking a small fraction of every trade. Usually the more you

trade, the fee rate decreases according to a published
fee schedule.

Pricing on Different Exchanges

Different exchanges can have different prices for each
cryptocurrency because of the different participants
using the exchange and supply and demand levels.
Usually, the prices are within a few percent of each
other. If they get too out of line, arbitrageurs step in
and buy the bitcoins from the exchange where they
are cheap and sell them where they are trading at
a premium.

To complete the circle of a successful arbitrage, you
need to move the fiat to the cheap exchange. Then, buy
bitcoins, withdraw them, and send them to the more
expensive exchange. Finally sell them, withdraw the
fiat, and repeat the cycle. Each step has a financial cost
and may not be instant. Therefore there can be price
differentials between exchanges for some time.

Regulation

Cryptocurrency exchanges perform activities that
may be regulated in their operational jurisdictions.
However, depending on how the legislation is written,

and owing to regulatory uncertainty, the classification of cryptocurrencies, exchanges currently operate in a legal grey area, especially crypto-only exchanges that allow trades between cryptocurrencies but not fiat.

Over-the-Counter (OTC) Brokers

When you buy on an exchange, you are buying from another exchange customer in quantities and prices agreed between you and the other customer. Every trade is shown to all other participants, and the order book moves in real-time in response to the trading activity. One characteristic of exchange trading that a large trader may wish to avoid is that transparency. Sometimes you want to trade large amounts without other traders knowing or moving the market.

Enter the brokers. Instead of showing a transparent order book of customer orders, the brokers will buy and sell directly with you, negotiating a price for the full amount you want to transact in what are known as "block trades." Trade details are not published to the public. Legitimate brokers also apply KYC processes to establish your identity and may be bound by local disclosure requirements.

When you trade with a broker, there are two modes: the broker could act as principal to the trade or as an agent.

When the broker acts as principal, the deal is between you and the broker. You tell them what you want to do (buy or sell) and in what amount, and they will tell you their best price. In accounting jargon, the trade is on the broker's balance sheet because the broker trades with you.

When the broker acts as an agent, the deal is between you and someone else. The broker acts as an intermediary. Generally, you contact the broker and tell them what you want to do; then the broker will try to find someone who wants to do the other side of the trade. The broker will communicate price and amount information to both sides until the deal is agreed. The broker takes a fee from one or both customers for this service.

Due to the large amount of manual overhead and small margins, brokers usually have a minimum trade size below which they won't pick up the phone; this can be anywhere from $10,000 to $100,000 per trade and increases as the market matures.

Localbitcoins

A website, localbitcoins.com, acts like eBay for cryptocurrencies. People post prices at which they are willing to buy and sell bitcoins. You can browse the list to find someone nearby and agree to send them money in return for bitcoins. It also has an escrow function for the temporary custody of cryptocurrency.

Who Is Satoshi Nakamoto?

Satoshi, author of the Bitcoin whitepaper, was active on cypherpunk mailing lists. After publishing the original whitepaper, Satoshi continued participating on Bitcoin forums until December 2013, then vanished.

Satoshi also owns or controls a significant number of bitcoins, estimated in 2013 by cryptocurrency security consultant Sergio Lerner at one million bitcoins. This represents just under 5 percent of the total 21 million bitcoins that will ever be created, if the protocol rules don't change. At $10,000 per Bitcoin (as of 2018), the bitcoins controlled by Satoshi are valued at ten billion dollars. If Satoshi moves any of this Bitcoin, the addresses thought to be associated with

Satoshi are monitored, and this would almost certainly affect the price of Bitcoin.

If the real creator(s) were discovered, they could dominate the future of Bitcoin. They would also have high personal security risks; it is not good for people to know that you have significant wealth, especially in cryptocurrency.

Several high-profile cryptocurrency owners publicly stated that they have sold all their cryptocurrencies. In January 2018, Charlee Lee, founder of Litecoin (LTC), and Steve Wozniak, founder of Apple, both publicly stated they (respectively) sold or donated all their LTC and Bitcoin.

There have been several high-profile attempts at exposing Satoshi's identity. Known in the industry as "doxxings": the public revelation of an internet nickname's real-world identity. It is highly unlikely that Satoshi's real identity is among these doxxings.

On March 14, 2014, a cover article for *Newsweek* magazine claimed that Satoshi was a sixty-four-year-old man named Dorian Nakamoto (birth name Satoshi Nakamoto) living in California.

The article included a photograph of Dorian's house. This led to repeated harassment of Dorian and his family. Of course, Dorian was not Satoshi. Identifying his home address is unethical. Nevertheless, anecdotal evidence suggests that Dorian is now enjoying his newfound fame as the real fake Satoshi.

In December 2015, an article in *WIRED* suggested that Dr. Craig Wright, an Australian computer scientist, could be the mastermind behind Bitcoin. In March 2016, in interviews with *GQ*, BBC, and *The Economist*, Craig claimed to be the leader of the Satoshi team. He even published a blog post, now taken offline, with these claims. Craig suggested he didn't want to self-doxx, and that there may have been external pressures on him. In June 2016, the *London Review of Books* published a long-form article where the journalist, Andrew O'Hagan, was able to spend an extended amount of time with Craig Wright. This is well worth a read in full, and my favourite part is:

> Weeks later, I was in the kitchen of the house Wright was renting in London drinking tea with him when I noticed a book on the worktop called *Visions of Virtue in Tokugawa Japan*. I'd done some mugging up by then and was keen to nail the name thing.

"So that's where you say you got the Nakamoto part?" I asked. "From the eighteenth-century iconoclast who criticised all the beliefs of his time?"

"Yes."

"What about Satoshi?"

"It means 'Ash,' " he said. "The philosophy of Nakamoto is the neutral central path in trade. Our current system needs to be burned down and remade. That is what cryptocurrency does—it is the phoenix…"

"So, Satoshi is the ash from which the phoenix…"

"Yes. And Ash is also the name of a silly Pokémon character. The guy with Pikachu." Wright smiled. "In Japan the name of Ash is Satoshi," he said.

"So, basically, you named the father of Bitcoin after Pikachu's chum?"

"Yes," he said. "That'll annoy the buggery out of a few people."

Alas, the cryptographic proofs and demonstrations that Dr. Wright performed on and off camera were not

watertight, and the community is still undecided about
the veracity of his claims.

Other Satoshi suspects are PGP developer Hal
Finney, Bit gold inventor Nick Szabo, creator of
b-money Wei Dai, e-donkey, Mt Gox, and Stellar
creator Jed McCaleb, and Dave Kleiman. CoinDesk
has a more extensive list of those suspected to
be Satoshi.

Satoshi Nakamoto may be a pseudonym for a
group of people wishing to remain anonymous. Craig
Wright may have been part of that team. The team
may not even know each other's real-world identities.
We may get another clue in 2020 when the roughly
one million BTC locked in the Tulip Trust will be
accessible. The Tulip Trust is a trust fund supposedly
created by Dave Kleiman, an associate of Satoshi. It
contains early bitcoins Satoshi potentially owned.

People seem to have forgotten: A digital signature
proves possession and use of a private key, but
private keys can be shared among multiple people.
Private keys can also be lost. An email address can be
shared. A whitepaper can be written collaboratively,
so grammatical clues simply reveal the habits of the
editor. It is hard to tie the identity of an individual to
the author of a paper.

Chapter 3

ETHEREUM

What Is Ethereum?

Ethereum's vision is to create a censorship-resistant, self-sustaining, decentralised world computer. If you consider Bitcoin as trustless validation and distributed storage of (transaction) data, Ethereum is trustless validation and distributed storage and processing of data and logic.

Ethereum has a public blockchain running on 15,000 computers and the token on the blockchain is called Ether, currently the second most popular cryptocurrency.

Like Bitcoin, Ethereum is also a bunch of protocols run as Ethereum software that creates Ethereum transactions recorded on Ethereum's blockchain. In contrast with Bitcoin, Ethereum transactions can contain more than payment data, and the nodes in Ethereum can validate and process more than simple payments.

On Ethereum, you can submit transactions that create smart contracts—small bits of logic stored on Ethereum's blockchain on all the Ethereum nodes. These smart contracts can be invoked by sending Ether to them.

There are also forks of Ethereum, such as Ethereum Classic, which is also a public blockchain. Each fork has a separate coin (Ethereum using ETH, Ethereum Classic using ETC). The forks have a shared history with Ethereum up to a certain point in time, after which the blockchains differ (we will discuss forks later).

Ethereum's code can also be run as a private network, starting a new blockchain with limited participants.

How Do You Run Ethereum?

To participate in the Ethereum network, you can download some software called an Ethereum client, or you can write some yourself. The Ethereum client connects over the internet to other people's computers and starts downloading the Ethereum blockchain. It will also independently validate that each block conforms to the Ethereum protocol rules.

What does the Ethereum client software do? You can use it to:

- Connect to the Ethereum network

- Validate transactions and blocks

- Create new transactions and smart contracts

- Run smart contracts

- Mine for new blocks

Your computer becomes a "node" on the network, running an Ethereum Virtual Machine, and behaves equivalently to all the other nodes. Remember in a peer-to-peer network there is no "master" server, and each computer is equivalent in status to any other.

How Is Ethereum Similar to Bitcoin?

Ethereum Has an Inbuilt Cryptocurrency

Ethereum's token is called Ether, shortened to ETH. This is a cryptocurrency that can be traded for other cryptocurrencies or other sovereign currencies like BTC. ETH ownership is tracked on the Ethereum blockchain.

Ethereum Has a Blockchain

Like Bitcoin, Ethereum has a blockchain that contains transactions and smart contracts. The blocks are mined by some participants and distributed to other participants who validate them. You can explore this blockchain on etherscan.io.

Like Bitcoin, Ethereum blocks form a chain by referring to the hash of the previous block.

Ethereum Is Public and Permissionless

Anyone can download or write some software to connect to the network and start creating transactions and smart contracts, validating them, and mining blocks without needing to log in or sign up with any other organisation.

Like Bitcoin, you can take Ethereum software, modify it slightly, and create private networks that are not connected to the main public network. The private tokens and smart contracts won't be compatible with the public tokens, though, just like private Bitcoin networks.

Ethereum Has Proof-of-Work (PoW) Mining

Like Bitcoin, Ethereum has a PoW maths challenge called Ethash. Though, it is deliberately designed to reduce the efficiency edge of specialised ACIS chips. Common hardware is allowed to compete efficiently, allowing for greater decentralisation of miners. In practice though, specialised hardware has been created and so most blocks in Ethereum are created by one of a small group of miners.

Ethereum's plans to move from electricity-expensive, proof-of-work mining to a more energy-efficient, proof-of-stake mining protocol called Casper in a future release of the Ethereum software called Serenity. Proof-of-stake is a mining protocol in which your chance of creating a valid block is proportional to the number of coins (ETH) in your mining wallet.

Miners would no longer need to consume electricity competitively to win blocks. Proof-of-stake is possibly less democratic because those who already have accumulated a lot of ETH will have a higher chance of winning more blocks. New money will flow toward the wealthy, increasing the Gini coefficient of Ethereum holders.

With proof-of-work, the high capital costs and expertise required mean only a small minority of people can make money mining. With proof-of-stake, every ETH has an identical chance of winning a block, so you can get started with much less capital. This would also reduce the negative externalities of pollution caused by proof-of-work, which is a decent and honourable goal.

How Is Ethereum Different from Bitcoin?

This is where it gets more technical, and in many ways, more complex.

The Ethereum Virtual Machine Can Run Smart Contracts

The Ethereum software creates and starts a segregated virtual computer on your machine called an "Ethereum Virtual Machine" (EVM), processing all the Ethereum transactions and blocks and keeping track of all the account balances and results of the smart contracts. Each node on the Ethereum network runs the same EVM and processes the same data. Ethereum can be described as a replicated state machine because all the nodes running Ethereum come to a consensus about the state of the Ethereum Virtual Machine.

Compared with Bitcoin's primitive scripting language, the code that can be deployed in Ethereum and run as smart contracts is more advanced and approachable for developers. We will describe smart contracts in more detail later, but for now you can think of smart contracts as pieces of code run by all the nodes in Ethereum's Virtual Machine.

Gas

In Bitcoin, you can add a small amount of BTC as a transaction fee to the miner who successfully mines the block. Likewise, in Ethereum, you can add a small amount of ETH as a mining fee that goes to the miner who successfully mines the block.

The complication with Ethereum is that there are more types of transactions with different computational complexities. Ethereum has a concept of "gas," which is a price list based on the computational complexity of the different operations you instruct the miners to make in your transaction.

A basic transfer of ETH from one account to another uses 21,000 gas. Uploading and running smart contracts uses more gas depending on their complexity. When you submit an Ethereum transaction, you specify how much ETH you are willing to pay per gas used and a maximum gas limit.

Mining fee (in ETH) = gas price (in ETH per gas) x gas consumed (in gas).

Gas Price

The gas price is the amount of ETH you are prepared to pay per unit of gas for the transaction to be processed. As with Bitcoin transaction fees, this is a competitive market, and in general the busier the network, the higher the gas price people are willing to pay. In times of great demand for gas, prices spike.

Peaks are usually related to popular Initial Coin Offerings (ICOs), where many people attempt to send ETH to ICO smart contracts. The peak in December 2017 is related to the popular *CryptoKitties* Ethereum game. In 2018, the normal range for gas prices was between 0.000000005 ETH (5 GWei) and 0.000000020 ETH (20 GWei) per gas.

Gas Limit

The gas limit you set provides a ceiling for how much gas you are prepared for a transaction to consume. This stops you from over-paying if you accidentally submitted a complex transaction that you thought was simple. The miner will execute the transaction and charge you the amount of gas taken multiplied by the gas price you specified.

If you set the gas limit below the amount of gas it takes to process the transaction, the transaction will fail, and you will not be refunded your mining fee.

ETH Units

Just like one dollar can be split into a hundred cents, a BTC can be split into 100,000,000 Satoshi, and Ethereum too has its own unit-naming convention.

The smallest unit is a Wei, and there are 1,000,000,000,000,000,000 of them per ETH. There are also some other intermediate names: Finney, Szabo, Shannon, Lovelace, Babbage, and Ada—all named after people who made significant contributions to fields related to cryptocurrencies or networks.

Wei is usually used for a gas price (a gas price of two to fifty Giga-Wei per gas is common, where one GWei is 1,000,000,000 Wei).

Units in Ethereum		
Unit	Number per ETH	Most appropriate uses
Ether (ETH)	1	Currently used to denominate transaction amounts (eg 20 ETH) and mining rewards (5 ETH)
finney	1,000	
szabo	1,000,000	Currently the best unit for the cost of a basic transaction, eg 500 szabo
Gwei	1,000,000,000	Currently the best unit for Gas Prices eg 22 Gwei
Mwei	1,000,000,000,000	
Kwei	1,000,000,000,000,000	
wei	1,000,000,000,000,000,000	The base indivisible unit used by programmers

Ethereum's Block Time Is Shorter

In Ethereum, the time between blocks is around fourteen seconds, compared with Bitcoin's ten-ish minutes. You could say Bitcoin writes to its database roughly every ten minutes, whereas Ethereum writes to its database roughly every fourteen seconds.

Ethereum Has Smaller Blocks

Currently, Bitcoin's blocks are a little under a MB in size, whereas Ethereum blocks are fifteen to twenty KB. While Bitcoin's maximum block size is specified in bytes, Ethereum's block size is based on a complexity of contracts run, a gas limit per block, and the maximum is allowed to vary slightly from block to block.

Currently, the maximum block size in Ethereum is around eight million gas. You can fit around 380 basic transactions into a block (8,000,000 / 21,000). In Bitcoin, you currently get 1,500–2,000 basic transactions in a one-MB block.

Uncles: Blocks that Don't Quite Make It

Because Ethereum's block generation rate is much higher than Bitcoin's, the rate of "block clashes" increases. Multiple valid blocks can be created almost simultaneously, but only one can make it into the main chain.

In Ethereum, these leftover blocks are called uncles. Uncles can be referenced by a few of the subsequent blocks and although the data in them is not used, the slightly smaller reward for mining them is still valid.

This achieves two important things:

1. It incentivises miners to mine even though there is a high chance of creating a non-mainchain block

2. It increases the security of the blockchain by acknowledging the energy spent creating the uncle blocks

Transactions that end up in orphaned blocks are re-mined on the main chain. They don't cost the user more gas because the transaction in the orphaned block is treated as if it was never processed.

Accounts

Bitcoin uses the word address to describe accounts. Ethereum uses the word account but technically they are also addresses. The words seem to be more interchangeable with Ethereum.

Maybe you can say, "What's the address of your Ethereum account?" It doesn't matter.

There are two types of Ethereum accounts:

1. Accounts that only store ETH

2.   Accounts that contain smart contracts

Accounts that only store ETH are like Bitcoin addresses and are sometimes known as externally owned accounts. You make payments from these accounts by signing transactions with the appropriate private key. An example of an account that stores ETH is 0x2d7c76202834a11a99576acf2ca95a7e66928ba0.

Accounts that contain smart contracts are activated by a transaction sending ETH into them. Once the smart contract has been uploaded, it sits at an address, waiting to be used. An example of an account that has a smart contract is 0xcbe1060ee68bc0fed3c00f13d6f110b7eb6 434f6.

ETH Token Issuance

The issuance of Ether tokens is more complicated than Bitcoin. The number of ETH in existence are: Pre-mine + Block rewards + Uncle rewards.

Pre-Mine

Around seventy-two million ETH were created for the crowd sale in July/August 2014. This is sometimes called a "pre-mine," as they were written in rather than mined through proof-of-work hashing. These were distributed to initial project supporters and the project team itself. It was decided that after the initial crowd sale, future ETH generation would be capped at 25 percent of the pre-mine total, i.e., no more than eighteen million ETH could be mined per year.

Block Rewards

Originally, each block mined created five fresh ETH as the block reward. Due to concerns about oversupply, this was reduced to three ETH in a set of changes to the protocol called the Byzantium update in October 2017 (block 4,370,000).

Uncle Rewards

Some blocks are mined but do not form part of the main blockchain. In Bitcoin, these are called "orphans" and are entirely discarded, and the miner of the orphaned block receives no rewards. In Ethereum, these discarded blocks are called "uncles" and can be referenced by later blocks. If a later block references an uncle, the miner of the uncle gets some ETH. This is called the "uncle" reward. The miner of the later block

referencing the uncle also gets an additional small
reward called an "uncle referencing" reward.

The uncle reward used to be 4.375 ETH (7/8 of the
full 5 ETH reward). It was reduced in the Byzantium
upgrade to 0.625–2.625 ETH.

The biggest difference between ETH and BTC
token generation is that BTC generation has a planned
finite cap, whereas ETH generation continues
to be generated indefinitely. However, this rule
can be changed if the majority of the Ethereum
network agrees.

The Future of ETH Generation

The Ethereum community hasn't yet agreed on what
happens to the rate of issue when Ethereum moves
from proof-of-work to proof-of-stake. Some argue
that perhaps the rate at which ETH is created should
decrease, as the value will not have to subsidise
competitive electricity usage.

Mining Rewards

In Ethereum, the block miner receives the block and
uncle referencing rewards (new ETH), plus mining

fees (gas amount x gas price) from transactions and contracts run during the block.

Other Parts to Ethereum: Swarm and Whisper

For Ethereum to realise its vision as an unstoppable, censorship-resistant, self-sustaining, decentralised, "world" computer, it needs to calculate, store data, and communicate efficiently and robustly. The Ethereum Virtual Machine is one component of the whole, the element that does the decentralised calculations.

Swarm is another component. This is for peer-to-peer file sharing, like BitTorrent, but incentivised with micropayments of ETH. Files are split into chunks, distributed, and stored with participating volunteers. These nodes that store and serve the chunks are compensated with ETH from those storing and retrieving the data.

Whisper is an encrypted messaging protocol that allows nodes to send messages directly to each other in a secure way and that also hides the sender and receiver from third-party snoopers.

Governance

Vitalik Buterin, the creator of Ethereum, is hugely influential, and his opinions count, although he can't stop his creation or censor transactions or participants. For instance, he championed a hard fork to recover funds stolen in the DAO hack (this is explained later). Bitcoin, on the other hand, has a few influential developers, but nothing like Vitalik has with Ethereum. Nick Tomaino argues in a blog post that the governance of blockchains "may prove to be as important as the computer science and economics of blockchains." Whether a single influencer is good or bad for decentralised cryptocurrency networks is still to be determined.

Smart Contracts

Smart contracts mean different things depending on the blockchain platform. Ethereum smart contracts are short computer programs stored on Ethereum's blockchain, replicated across all the nodes, and available for anyone to inspect. Two steps are performed separately:

1. Uploading the smart contract to
    Ethereum's blockchain

2. Making the smart contract run

You upload a smart contract by sending a special transaction to miners. If the transaction is successfully processed, the smart contract will then exist at a specific address on Ethereum's blockchain.

For a real example of a smart contract, the smart contract that holds the balances of the Indorse ICO tokens can be found at address 0xf8e386eda857484f5a12e4b5daa9984e06e73705.

When you want to run the smart contract, you create a transaction pointing to the contract and supply whatever information the contract expects. You pay gas to the miner to run it. As part of the mining process, each miner will execute the transaction, which involves running the smart contract.

The miner who successfully wins the proof-of-work challenge will publish the winning block to the rest of the network. The other nodes will validate the block, add the block to their blockchains, and process the transactions, including running the smart contracts. This is how Ethereum's blockchain gets updated and how the state of the EVMs on each node's machine is synchronised.

Ethereum smart contracts are described as "Turing complete." This means they are fully functional and can perform any computation that can be done in any other programming language.

Smart Contract languages: Solidity / Serpent, LLL (Lisp-Like Language)

The most common language that Ethereum smart contracts are written in is Solidity. Serpent and LLL can also be used. Smart contracts written in these languages will all compile and run on Ethereum Virtual Machines.

- Solidity, currently the most popular, is like the language JavaScript.

- Serpent, popular early on in Ethereum's history, is like the language Python.

- LLL is like Lisp and was used in the early days only. It is probably the hardest to write.

Ethereum Software: Geth, Eth, Pyethapp

The three official Ethereum clients (full node software) are all open source. You can see the code behind them and tweak them to make your own versions. They are:

- geth (written in a language called Go)

- eth (written in C++)

- pyethapp (written in Python)

These are all command-line green-text-based programs, and additional software can be used for a graphical interface. Currently, the most popular graphical interface is Mist, which runs on top of geth or eth.

Currently the most popular Ethereum clients are geth and Parity. Parity is an open-source Ethereum software developed in the Rust programming language and built by a company called Parity Technologies.

Ethereum's History

Ethereum is a highly successful public blockchain by adoption, mindshare, and the number of developers working on Ethereum smart contracts and decentralised apps. Below is a short history of Ethereum and some difficult periods in its history that it has managed to overcome.

2013

Vitalik Buterin described Ethereum as a concept in a white paper in late 2013. This concept was developed by Dr. Gavin Wood, who published a technical yellow paper in April 2014. Since then, the development of Ethereum's software has been managed by a community of developers.

A crowd sale took place in July and August 2014 to fund development, and Ethereum's live blockchain was launched on July 30, 2015. You can see the first block here: etherscan.io/block/0.

Ethereum Crowd Sale

The development team was funded by an online sale of ETH tokens from July to August 2014, where people could buy ETH tokens by paying in Bitcoin. Early investors received 2,000 ETH per BTC, gradually reducing to 1,337 ETH per BTC over about a month to encourage investors to invest early.

Crowd sale participants sent bitcoins to a Bitcoin address and received an Ethereum wallet containing the number of ETH bought. Technical details are on Ethereum's blog.

A little over sixty million ETH was sold this way for more than 31,500 BTC, worth about eighteen million US dollars at the time. An additional 20 percent (twelve million ETH) were created to fund development and the Ethereum Foundation.

Software Release Codenames

Frontier, Homestead, Metropolis, and Serenity are friendly names for versions of the core Ethereum software, like Apple's OS X version names such as Mavericks, El Capitan, and Sierra.

Release name	Details
Olympic (testnet)	Launched May 2015–a testing release where coins are not compatible with 'real' ETH. A testnet still runs in parallel to the main live network so that developers can test their code. The testnet operates in the same way as the live network but there is much less mining competition as the coins are not tradeable on exchanges–they are defined has having zero value.
Frontier	Launched 30 July 2015–an initial live release with a way for people to mine ETH and build and run contracts.

Homestead	Launched 14 March 2016–some protocol changes, more stability.
Metropolis	This was designed to prepare Ethereum for a move from proof-of-work to proof-of-stake. Metropolis was split into two upgrades, Byzantium and Constantinople. Byzantium was released in October 2017 at block 4,370,000. It included changes to set the stage for private transactions, sped up transaction processing (important for scalability), and improved some smart contract functionality. The most visually obvious change was reducing the mining reward from 5 ETH per block to 3 ETH. The Constantinople upgrade will be another upgrade to set the stage for the move to proof-of-stake (Casper).
Serenity	Future launch–moving from proof-of-work to proof-of-stake (Casper).

The DAO Hack

A "decentralised autonomous organisation" is an automated company or entity that runs itself according to some encoded charter, without human intervention.

In 2016, Slock-it, a German company, pivoted from making smart locks opened by using tokens on blockchains and built an automated venture capital (VC) company as a smart contract on Ethereum's public blockchain. They called it "The DAO" (note the capitalisation), which is like calling a bank "The Bank." Anyway, The DAO is an example of a DAO.

The DAO's idea was a cryptocurrency that funded start-ups: investors would send money (in ETH), like a traditional VC fund. The smart contract would issue them DAO tokens in proportion to their investment.

In a normal VC fund, the investors, called Limited Partners, expect the VC firm to manage given funds to generate a return by investing in successful ventures. DAO tokens would be used to vote on what start-ups receive funding instead of a management team deciding. The smart contract would govern a voting process, and, at the end of a vote, cryptocurrency would be released to the start-ups that had the most funding votes.

A management team had to curate a list of potential start-ups to vote on—not much of a DAO after all. All it did was automate the provision of funds, and the DAO failed before it invested in a single start-up.

In May 2016, The DAO managed to raise the equivalent of over $150 million USD in ETH. The DAO held about 15 percent of all ETH in existence.

In June, a hacker managed to find a way to get The DAO to release 3,641,694 ETH (about fifty to sixty million dollars) to the hacker's account by exploiting a bug in The DAO smart contract, sending the price of ETH down almost 50 percent. When the hack was discovered and investigated, some "ethical" hackers drained the rest of the ETH into their accounts.

The Ethereum Foundation suggested an update that would freeze the drained ETH, blacklisting the hacker's account. A bug was found with the proposed change, so the blacklist wasn't adopted. The Ethereum Foundation then made a proposal to unwind and allow DAO investors to withdraw their invested ETH.

In July 2016, a vote was taken, and the community installed an upgrade known as a hard fork that would move the stolen Ether to a new smart contract and have them returned to the original investors.

An unstoppable immutable world computer was stopped and mutated to cater to a small number of people who lost a lot of money to a smart contract that functioned as specified.

Ethereum Classic

A small community continued with the old Ethereum software. One blockchain returned the stolen funds to The DAO investors and another didn't, now known as Ethereum Classic. Ethereum and Ethereum Classic have a shared history until block 1,920,000 (July 2016). Anyone who owned ETH before the fork now had an equal amount of ETH (tokens recorded on the Ethereum blockchain) and ETC (tokens recorded on the Ethereum Classic blockchain). This was good for anyone who had ETH before the hard fork as they functionally received free money in the form of ETC.

The Parity Bug

Parity is a piece of Ethereum software written by Parity Technologies. It acts as a full node on the Ethereum network, storing the blockchain, running contracts, forwarding transactions, etc. At the time of writing, about a third of Ethereum nodes run Parity software. Parity also contains wallet software.

On July 20, 2017, Parity was updated to fix a bug that enabled a hacker to steal thirty-two million dollars' worth of ETH from Parity multi-signature wallets. In that update, a smart contract was deployed that had a vulnerability. Anyone could convert this smart contract into a multi-signature wallet, take ownership of it, and then suicide it. Multi-signature wallets created after July 20 relied on that smart contract, freezing the assets in the wallets.

So, someone with the GitHub handle devops199 "did just that on 6 Nov 2017:"

Anyone can kill your contract #6995

I accidentally killed it.

etherscan.io/address/
0x863df3bfa4469f3ead0be8f912ase51c91a907b4

Almost six hundred wallets were affected, with a combined balance of about $150 million of ETH. Gavin Wood, founder of Parity Technologies, had about 300,000 ETH in a Parity wallet. Those funds are frozen.

The ETH are still there in the wallets, but currently can't be sent. As of early 2018, developers are still investigating if anything can be done to fix this bug.

Actors in the Ethereum Ecosystem

The Ethereum Foundation

The Ethereum Foundation is a nonprofit organisation registered as "Stiftung Ethereum" in Switzerland whose mission is to:

*Promote and support Ethereum
platform and base layer research...to
produce next generation decentralised
applications (dapps), and together
build a more globally accessible, more
free and more trustworthy Internet.*

The foundation's job is to manage the funds raised in the Ether presale in any way that furthers Ethereum. It pays the core development team a salary and offers developers grants to tackle specific problems. Vitalik Buterin sits on the council's foundation, and the foundation influences the roadmap of Ethereum. In theory, Ethereum participants (miners, bookkeepers) don't have to implement any software changes the foundation makes, but in practice, they do.

Ethereum Enterprise Alliance

The Ethereum Enterprise Alliance is a nonprofit group launched in March 2017 whose goal is to make Ethereum suitable for enterprise use. It is hard to understand whether this means businesses using the public Ethereum blockchain, or if it means adapting the Ethereum code to make it suitable for industry use cases.

The website says:

> The Enterprise Ethereum Alliance connects
> Fortune 500 enterprises, start-ups, academics,
> and technology vendors with Ethereum subject
> matter experts... Ethereum—to define enterprise-
> grade software capable of handling the most
> complex, highly demanding applications at the
> speed of business.

From the website, the vision of the EEA is to:

- Be an open-source standard, not a product

- Address enterprise deployment requirements

- Evolve in tandem with advances in
  public Ethereum

- Leverage existing standards

Unfortunately, I could not find any further detail as to
what this means. The mission of the alliance states:

- EEA is a 501(c)(6) nonprofit corporation.

- A clear roadmap for enterprise features
  and requirements.

- Robust governance model and accountability,
  clarity around IP and licensing models for
  open-source technology.

- Resources for businesses to learn about
  Ethereum and leverage this groundbreaking
  technology to address specific industry
  use cases.

Its members are an impressive list of large
established companies and new start-ups. The launch
members included:

- Accenture
- Amis
- BBVA
- BlockApps
- BP
- Brainbot
- BNY Mellon
- CME Group
- Chronicled
- Intel

- JP Morgan
- Meta
- Microsoft
- Tendermint
- Telindus
- Santander
- String
- UBS
- Wipro

Members pay between $3,000 and $25,000 in annual
dues for benefits, including:

- May create and participate in working group

- Have access to open code

- Included in new member press releases

- Offered discount on EEA sponsorships

- Invited to all member meetings

- Company logo hosted on EEA website

The EEA website also explains why prospective
members should join the EEA:

> The EEA is an industry-supported, not-for-
> profit established to build, promote, and
> broadly support Ethereum-based technology
> best practices, open standards, and open-
> source reference architectures. The EEA is
> helping to evolve Ethereum into an enterprise-
> grade technology, providing research and
> development in a range of areas, including
> privacy, confidentiality, scalability, and security.
> The EEA is also investigating hybrid architectures
> that span both permissioned and public
> Ethereum networks as well as industry-specific
> application layer working groups.

In early 2018, there were 450 members according to a
CoinDesk article.

Ether Price

Like Bitcoin, the price of Ether has also been through
ups and downs. Ethereum's crowd sale was at a price of
two thousand ETH to one BTC, and at the time (July–
August 2014), a BTC was worth about five hundred
dollars, making one ETH worth twenty-five cents. At
its peak in early 2018, the price of ETH almost touched
$1,500. So, to date, Ether has been a highly successful
cryptocurrency in terms of price.

Compared to Bitcoin, Ethereum has an additional
use case. Its token ETH is often used in ICOs. A
company that runs an ICO will create a smart contract
on Ethereum that will automatically create tokens
and assign them to Ethereum addresses that have
sent Ether to a related smart contract. This means
you can run an automated ICO on Ethereum as long
as investors pay in ETH or another token recorded
on Ethereum.

Chapter 4

FORKS

What is a cryptocurrency fork? When people use the word *fork*, it can mean two different but related things:

1. A fork of a codebase
2. A fork of a live blockchain (a chainsplit)

The difference is whether you're creating an entirely new ledger, achieved by forking a codebase (the code behind the node software), or creating a new coin that has a shared history with an existing coin by forking a blockchain.

A Fork of a Codebase

A fork of a codebase is where you copy the code of a particular program so you can contribute to it or adapt it. This is encouraged in open-source software, where code is deliberately shared for anyone to tinker with.

In cryptocurrency, you copy the code behind a popular cryptocurrency node software, change a few parameters, and then run the code to create an entirely new blockchain starting from a blank ledger. You'd say you forked Bitcoin's code to create a new coin. This is how many altcoins (alternative coins) were created in 2013–14. Litecoin was created using a copy of Bitcoin's code with some parameters changed, including the speed of block generation and the kind of calculations the miners had to do in the proof-of-work challenge.

In the popular open-source code-sharing platform GitHub, you can easily fork (copy) a project's code with a few clicks of a mouse. You then have a copy that you can edit. These codebase forks are common and encouraged in open-source technology development, as they lead to innovation.

A Fork of a Live Blockchain: Chainsplits

A fork of a live blockchain, better described as a *chainsplit*, is more interesting and can happen accidentally or on purpose.

An accidental chainsplit is when there is an uncontentious software upgrade and some of the network omits or forgets to upgrade their software, leading to several blocks being produced that are incompatible with the rest of the network. According to BitMEX research, this has happened a few times in Bitcoin's history, with three identified chainsplits lasting approximately fifty-one, twenty-four, and six blocks in 2010, 2013, and 2015, respectively. So forks can occur even when there is no contention over rule changes.

Accidental chainsplits tend to be resolved quickly with the small proportion of participants upgrading their software and discarding the incompatible blocks.

A deliberate chainsplit occurs when a group of network participants thinks things should be done differently and runs some new software with new protocols to create a new coin with a shared history with the old coin. Deliberate chainsplits can be successful, with both assets continuing to live and develop, or fail, not having enough interest and the value of the token drops to zero and stops being mined.

To execute a successful deliberate chainsplit, you need to persuade a group of miners, bookkeepers, exchanges, and wallets that your new rules are better than the existing rules. They will need to agree to support your new coin, creating a community supporting a new coin that people can buy and sell and store and use. When the chain splits, you create a new coin with different protocol rules but share a history with the original coin. Anyone with a balance on the blockchain before the split now has a balance in two different coins after the split.

So the determination of whether something is a protocol upgrade, a failed fork, or a successful fork is about who chooses to adopt the new rules.

- If new protocol rules are adopted by most of the community, then it is called a protocol upgrade, and those who don't upgrade have a choice to maintain the old rules as an attempted fork or to join the majority.

- If few participants adopt new protocol rules, you have an unviable fork, which may ultimately fail.

- If enough participants adopt new protocol rules to maintain a community and interest, it is a successful fork.

What's the Result of a Deliberate, Successful Fork?

The upshot is that anyone who owned some of the original cryptocurrency continues to have the original cryptocurrency, plus the same number of tokens in the new forked cryptocurrency.

If coin holders had a hundred tokens before a successful cryptocurrency fork, have they "doubled their money"? In one sense, yes, as they now have a hundred units of the old coin and a hundred units of the new coin, and they can spend them independently. The two coins have different fiat currency values. In practice, the old currency tends to maintain its fiat value, whereas the new one must float on exchanges with a new ticker symbol, and it will usually start trading at a lower value.

How Does a Deliberate Chainsplit Work?

Participants of a fork change the protocol rules and market their philosophy to a wide audience of miners, wallet software providers, exchanges, merchants, and users. They then coordinate to switch over to the new rules at a planned time, determined by a specific block number known as a block height.

At that planned time, two incompatible blocks are mined, one valid for the incumbent participants and the other for the rebellious participants. The blockchain splits into two.

So now there are two blockchains. The coins will have different symbols and names to differentiate them, wallets need to be configured to accept the new coin, exchanges need to list the new coin to create a market for it, and merchants and other participants need to accept the new coin.

Media Descriptions

Forks, specifically chainsplits, are often described in the media as a "stock split." This is a poor analogy because, in a stock split, more shares are created and assigned to shareholders, but the old and new shares all represent the same thing. A "spinoff" is a more accurate analogy because, in a spinoff, shareholders of the old company get new shares of a new company. This is like a fork where holders of the original coin also get the new coin with different rules from the old coin.

Hard Forks vs. Soft Forks

Sometimes the terms *hard* and *soft fork* are used. These terms refer to changes in the rules about what constitutes a valid transaction and block.

A soft fork is a change in the rules that is backward compatible, meaning that blocks created under the newly changed rules will still be considered valid by participants who didn't upgrade.

A hard fork is a change in the rules that is not backward compatible, so if some participants fail to upgrade, there will be a chainsplit.

In practice, if changes to protocol rules are tightened or more constrained, this results in a soft fork, whereas if consensus rules are loosened, then this is a hard fork.

Case Study One: Bitcoin Cash

Bitcoin Cash is a (currently) successful fork of Bitcoin, created as a hard fork. Bitcoin Cash and Bitcoin (sometimes called Bitcoin Core to reduce confusion) had a shared history until block 478,558, when the chain split.

The philosophy of Bitcoin Cash is to more accurately reflect the vision in the original Satoshi whitepaper of fast, cheap, decentralised, censorship-resistant digital cash, and proponents believe that Bitcoin Core has not made progress toward this vision.

So far, Bitcoin Cash has been regarded as successful, as it is supported by popular wallet software, merchants accept it, and it trades on popular cryptocurrency exchanges under the ticker symbol BCH.

Case Study Two: Ethereum Classic

Ethereum Classic is a (currently) successful fork of Ethereum. It was created, as we saw earlier, after The DAO was hacked and more than fifty million dollars of ETH was drained from it. The Ethereum community deliberated, and the majority decided to hard fork at block 1,920,000 and restored the hacked ETH to the original holders.

But a minority of the community saw this restoration as revisionist and anti-ethical and refused to hard fork, so they continued with the original blockchain, theft and all.

Ethereum Classic trades on cryptocurrency exchanges under the ticker symbol ETC and is widely supported by wallets.

Other Forks

It is easier to take something that has already worked than to build something from scratch. And, as cryptocurrencies tend to be open-source, it is legal to copy the code, tweak it, and run it. Community building with a forked chain is easier than building a new blockchain. Anyone who had a balance on the original chain will also have a balance on the new chain, so they are more likely to support a fork where they have a balance rather than a new blank blockchain.

People saw that Bitcoin Cash successfully forked and retained some currency value, so others tried the same. However, there is only so much energy in the cryptocurrency space, and there seems to be some "fork fatigue." Over forty forks have developed since the Bitcoin Cash fork.

Chapter 5

BLOCKCHAIN TECHNOLOGY

What Is Blockchain Technology?

You will see the phrase "blockchain technology" and "blockchain" in many different contexts, and different people use the words to mean different things. Angela Walch, research fellow at University College London, provides commentary in her 2017 paper "The Path of the Blockchain Lexicon (and the Law)." In this chapter, I will briefly overview of blockchain technology and explain some nuances.

By now, you should understand that there is no such thing as "the blockchain," just as there is no such thing as "the database." ETH is the Ethereum blockchain, but you can create private Ethereum blockchains by running and connecting node software on some machines to each other. Your private Ethereum network will function like the public network, though your private ETH will not be compatible with the public ETH because it has a different history from the public version.

In print, if you read "the blockchain," you may need to guess what the writer means. In conversation, ask, "Which blockchain platform?" then, "The public chain or a private one?"

Blockchains fall under the broader category of "distributed ledgers." All blockchains are distributed ledgers, but not all distributed ledgers are blockchains. Sometimes journalists and consultants use "blockchain" to describe non-blockchain distributed ledgers.

We need to differentiate between blockchain technologies and specific blockchain ledgers.

Blockchain technologies are the rules or standards for creating and maintaining a ledger. When a network is created, the blockchain or ledger of record is initially empty of transactions. Some example blockchain technologies are Bitcoin, Ethereum, NXT, Corda, Fabric, and Quorum.

You may have heard of a few types or flavours of databases—Oracle databases, MySQL databases, etc., though they all have similar goals: efficient storage, sorting, and retrieval of data. Blockchains are similar. Some blockchain technologies operate one way, others operate differently, and you can have multiple instances of any blockchain technology in separate ledgers.

Public, Permissionless Blockchains

Public blockchains are permissionless because anyone may create blocks or be a bookkeeper without permission from an authority. In these public networks, anyone may create an address for receiving funds and create transactions for sending funds.

Private Instances of Public Blockchains

You could take and run the Ethereum code and point it to computers not on the public Ethereum network. As far as all these computers are concerned, they are starting with a fresh ledger with no entries.

Could you set up a small private network running Ethereum, then mine some ETH and transfer them to the public network? No. They have different records of account balances and therefore are incompatible. Nodes on each network can only validate what they see in their blockchain, and they cannot see coins on the other blockchain.

Permissioned (or Permissionable) Blockchains

Some platforms are designed to allow groups of participants to create blockchains in a private context. These are called "private blockchains" and are designed to only allow pre-approved participants to participate. Hence the term "permissioned."

Popular permissioned blockchains include:

- Corda, a platform built from scratch by R3 and a consortium of banks for use by regulated financial institutions but with broad applicability.

- Hyperledger Fabric, a platform built by IBM and donated to the Linux Foundation's Hyperledger Project. Fabric uses a concept of "channels" to restrict parties from seeing all transactions.

- Quorum, a private blockchain system based on Ethereum originally built by JP Morgan, uses advanced cryptographic constructs called *zero-knowledge proofs* to obfuscate data and address privacy issues.

- Various private instances of Ethereum under development by individual businesses.

Unlike permissionless networks such as Bitcoin and Ethereum, permissioned blockchains don't need a native token. They don't need to incentivise block-creators and don't need proof-of-work as the gating factor to write to the shared ledger. Instead, when businesses transact, they are looking for data that can be trusted to be up-to-date, agreed, and signed off by the appropriate parties. In a traditional business ecosystem, participants are all identified, and if some try to misbehave, they can be sued. When parties are identified and have legal agreements, the technical environment is not as hostile as that of the pseudonymous world of public cryptocurrency blockchains, where code is law, and there are no terms of service or legal agreements.

Some argue that permissioned private blockchains are somehow inferior to public cryptocurrency blockchains. Public cryptocurrency blockchains are like "the internet," open and permissionless, whereas private industry blockchains are closed like intranets. Basically, public blockchains will be successful and disruptive, whereas private blockchains are unsuccessful and not disruptive.

Intranets and private company networks are actually highly successful. And it is equally far from the truth to regard the internet as open and permissionless. As Tim Swanson notes on his blog in "Intranets and the Internet":

> The internet is actually a bunch of private networks of internet service providers (ISPs) that have legal agreements with the end users, cooperate through "peering" agreements with other ISPs, and communicate via a common, standardized routing protocols such as BGP which publishes autonomous system numbers.

Cryptocurrencies and private blockchains are different tools deployed to address different problems. They can happily coexist. Public and private blockchains will naturally operate in different ways. After all, technology is a tool, and tools exist to serve a need.

What Is Common to Blockchain Technologies?

Blockchains usually contain the following concepts:

1. A data store (database) that records changes in the data. You can store and record changes to any kind of data in a blockchain.

2. Replication of the data store across several systems in real-time. Bitcoin and Ethereum ensure that all data is sent to all participants: everyone sees everything. Other technologies are more selective about where data is sent.

3. "Peer to -peer" rather than client-server network architecture. Data may be "gossiped" to neighbours rather than broadcast by a single coordinator acting as the golden source of data.

4. Cryptographic methods such as digital signatures to prove ownership and authenticity, and hashes for references and sometimes to manage write-access.

I often describe blockchain technology as "a collection of technologies, a bit like a bag of Legos." You can take different bricks out of the bag and put them together differently to create different results.

Sometimes when discussing specific potential uses for this technology, we hear this exchange:

"But you don't need a blockchain to do that. You can use traditional technology!"

"So how would you do it?"

"Oh, some data storage, some peer-to-peer data-sharing, cryptography to ensure authenticity, hashes to ensure data tampering is evident, etc."

"But you've just described how blockchains work!"

So blockchains are not a new invention; instead, they put together existing technologies to create new capabilities.

What's the Difference Between a Blockchain and a Database?

A common database stores and retrieves data. A blockchain platform works the same way. It also connects to other peers, listens for new data, validates new data against pre-agreed rules, then stores and broadcasts that new data to other network participants constantly, without manual intervention.

What's the Difference between a Distributed Database and a Distributed Ledger?

Replicated databases are not new. Sharded databases, where the workload and storage are spread around multiple machines, usually to increase speed and storage, are also not new. However, with distributed ledgers or blockchains, participants do not need to trust each other. They do not work on the assumption that the other participants behave honestly, so each participant checks everything individually.

What Are Blockchains Good For?

The motivations between public and private blockchains are different. Let's consider them separately.

Public Blockchains

To date, public blockchains have been used with some success in the following areas:

1. Speculation

2. Darknet markets

3. Cross-border payments

4. Initial Coin Offerings

Speculation

The main use for cryptocurrencies is undoubtedly speculation. Their prices are volatile, and people make and lose a lot of money trading these coins.

There are no established methods to value a cryptocurrency, so prices will likely remain volatile. Financial markets use pricing models to constrain prices within broadly understood limits. Fiat currencies trade based on comparative economic data. Other traditional financial assets have other standardised pricing methodologies. Up to now, however, I have not seen credible methods for pricing cryptocurrencies or ICO tokens. As the industry matures, pricing models will be explored, and after some time become widely accepted.

Darknet Markets

Cryptocurrencies have been used with some success to buy items from underground marketplaces.

The traceability of certain cryptocurrencies makes them flawed candidates for illegal activity. In 2015, two undercover US federal agents from the Drug Enforcement Agency (DEA) and the US Secret Service allegedly stole, bribed, blackmailed, and laundered the proceeds while investigating the Silk Road drug marketplace. They were charged with money laundering and wire fraud. Here is an excerpt from a press release issued by the US Department of Justice:

> Carl M. Force, 46, of Baltimore, was a Special Agent with the DEA, and Shaun W. Bridges, 32, of Laurel, Maryland, was a Special Agent with the US Secret Service (USSS). Both were assigned to the Baltimore Silk Road Task Force, which investigated illegal activity in the Silk Road marketplace. Force served as an undercover agent and was tasked with establishing communications with a target of the investigation, Ross Ulbricht, a.k.a. "Dread Pirate Roberts." Force is charged with wire fraud, theft of government property, money laundering and conflict of interest. Bridges is charged with wire fraud and money laundering.
>
> According to the complaint, Force was a DEA agent assigned to investigate the Silk Road marketplace. During the investigation, Force engaged in certain authorized undercover operations by, among other things, communicating online with "Dread Pirate Roberts" (Ulbricht), the target of his investigation. The complaint alleges, however, that Force then, without authority, developed additional online

personas and engaged in a broad range of illegal activities calculated to bring him personal financial gain. In doing so, the complaint alleges, Force used fake online personas, and engaged in complex Bitcoin transactions to steal from the government and the targets of the investigation. Specifically, Force allegedly solicited and received digital currency as part of the investigation, but failed to report his receipt of the funds, and instead transferred the currency to his personal account. In one such transaction, Force allegedly sold information about the government's investigation to the target of the investigation. The complaint also alleges that Force invested in and worked for a digital currency exchange company while still working for the DEA, and that he directed the company to freeze a customer's account with no legal basis to do so, then transferred the customer's funds to his personal account. Further, Force allegedly sent an unauthorized Justice Department subpoena to an online payment service directing that it unfreeze his personal account.

Bridges allegedly diverted to his personal account over $800,000 in digital currency that he gained control of during the Silk Road investigation. The complaint alleges that Bridges

> placed the assets into an account at Mt. Gox, the now-defunct digital currency exchange in Japan. He then allegedly wired funds into one of his personal investment accounts in the United States mere days before he sought a $2.1 million seizure warrant for Mt. Gox's accounts.

On July 1, 2015, Force pled guilty to money laundering, wire fraud, theft of government property, obstruction of justice, and extortion. On August 31, 2015, Bridges pled guilty to money laundering and obstruction of justice.

As we can see, don't use bitcoins to perform or fund illegal activities.

Cross-Border Payments

While there may have been limited success in using cryptocurrencies as a vehicle to move fiat across borders, adoption has been limited. I attempted to send two hundred Singapore dollars to my friend in Indonesia using three methods: Western Union, bank transfer, and Bitcoin. The Bitcoin route was the worst user experience and the most expensive.

The core problem is that in a conventional fiat-to-fiat remittance, there is only one exchange of currencies. Using cryptocurrencies, there are now two exchanges: fiat to crypto, then crypto to fiat. More exchanges mean more steps, complexity, and cost.

Cross-border payments were initially trumpeted as a "killer app" for Bitcoin and cryptocurrencies, especially in 2014–15. Indeed, in June 2018, money transfer agency Western Union announced that they had been testing XRP for six months and had yet to see any savings. Perhaps the industry is in the "trough of disillusionment" in Gartner's technology hype cycle.

Initial Coin Offerings (ICOs)

ICOs are a new method of fundraising that became popular in 2016. Companies offer tokens to people in return for cryptocurrency. Tokens usually represent a claim on future goods or services provided by that company. We discuss ICOs in more detail in the next section.

Other

I have seen public blockchains being used for other "fringe" purposes, for example, storing hashes on a blockchain to prove that some data existed at a certain time. I haven't seen evidence that this use is particularly widespread.

Critics often claim cryptocurrencies are widely used for money laundering. While undoubtedly happens using cryptocurrencies, as there is with fiat currencies, it is unclear what proportion of global money laundering is performed through cryptocurrencies. For serious organised crime, I suspect that the cryptocurrency markets are too small and illiquid to satisfy their demands. Big business enterprises, high-value banknotes, and even banks are more likely to be the preferred vehicles for most money laundering.

Private Blockchains

While public blockchains have enabled censorship-resistant digital cash, they were not designed to solve the problems of traditional businesses.

Business-to-Business Communication

Processes within an organisation have been made efficient using internal systems, workflow tools, intranets, and data repositories. However, the sophistication of technology used to communicate between organisations has remained low. In some advanced situations, APIs (application programming interfaces) are used for machine-to-machine communications, but in most cases, we rely on emails, PDFs, and pieces of paper with wet-ink signatures to be couriered across the world.

Duplicative Data, Processes, and Reconciliation

Businesses trust their data but not anyone else's. This means that businesses within an ecosystem duplicate data and processes. Version control of documents and records is painful unless a third party is paid to be the golden source. Reconciliation only goes some way to solving these pain points.

Invoices could be a PDF created by someone at company A, perhaps signed off by someone else in company A before a copy is sent from the accounts receivable department to someone at company B. They save a copy on their hard drive and forward a copy to someone else. Another copy goes to the accounts payable department, and, when the invoice is paid, everyone needs to be updated. There could be ten or more copies of the invoice floating around, none of which are kept in sync. When the state of the invoice changes from "unpaid" to "paid," this is not reflected on all the copies of the invoice.

Private Blockchains

Businesses have become interested in concepts from public blockchains, such as unique digital assets and cryptographically secured ledger entries. However, the transparency of public blockchains is unattractive to businesses that may require a level of commercial confidentiality.

Private blockchains have been inspired by public blockchains but are being designed to meet the needs of business. Private blockchains do not need mechanisms such as energy-intensive proof-of-work mining.

Some technology inspired by public blockchains is more accurately called "distributed ledgers." Corda is an open-source platform like public blockchains, but it doesn't bundle transactions for batch processing and distribution across the whole network.

A key benefit of blockchains and similar data structures is that parties know that a set of statements is complete and that the statements themselves are complete and untampered. Each party can verify this.

Banks need to know their list of trades is complete
and the data within the trades is consistent with
their counterparty.

Private blockchains aim to increase the quality and
security of technology used in business-to-business
communications. They allow unique digital assets to
move freely and reliably between companies without
needing a third party to act as a record keeper. Private
blockchains can provide transparent multilateral
workflows in the form of smart contracts and
demonstrate that the agreed workflows are adhered
to. Instead of having to trust a business to perform as
agreed, a smart contract ensures that pre-programmed
processes are followed.

Private blockchains may be useful whenever a
business interacts with another business to share
workflows, processes, or assets. The wholesale
banking industry was the first to invest, understand,
and use this technology. Perhaps the fact that Bitcoin
was described as a cryptocurrency also made it
interesting to banks.

Imagine if the invoice were recorded on a ledger
that was kept in sync between both companies,
bilaterally, and as soon as it was approved, signed, or
paid, both parties would know about it, streamlining

many business processes. The concepts could be extended to any document, record, or data.

SWIFT and Bolero are examples of parties that store data and be the golden source. But a third party may not be viable since regulatory or geographical reasons prevent such a party's emergence. Industries can be suspicious of single points of power and control. So there are several reasons why having a third party may not be viable.

Non-financial industries are now exploring the technology for digital identity, supply chains, trade finance, healthcare, procurement, real estate, and asset registries.

Notable Private Blockchains

Some private or permissioned blockchains are certainly gaining mindshare and traction. Current examples are:

Axoni AxCore

Axoni is a capital market technology firm founded in 2013 that specialises in distributed ledger technology and blockchain infrastructure. Axoni's flagship initiative uses their technology to upgrade the

Depository Trust and Clearing Corporation's trade information warehouse.

R3 Corda

Corda is an open-source blockchain project designed to aid the financial services industry. It was designed by a consortium of banks and R3, my employer, so I declare my interest here. In Chief Technology Officer Richard Brown's words:

> Corda is an open-source enterprise blockchain platform that has been designed and built from the ground up to enable legal contracts and other shared data to be managed and synchronised between mutually untrusting organisations in any industry. Uniquely amongst enterprise blockchain platforms, Corda allows a diverse range of applications to interoperate on a single global network.

Corda uses concepts from Bitcoin and public blockchains to guarantee that digital assets are unique, and data is synchronised between different parties' databases. But it does not bundle unrelated transactions together and distributes blocks through the network, instead processing higher transaction volumes and resolving the privacy issue of public blockchains.

Corda is used, among other things, for trading baskets of financial assets, gold trading, syndicated loans, and FX trade matching.

Digital Asset GSL

Digital Asset Holdings, LLC is a company founded in 2014. According to Wikipedia, it "Builds products based on distributed ledger technology (DLT) for regulated financial institutions, such as financial market infrastructure providers, CCPs, CSDs, exchanges, banks, custodians and their market participants." The technology platform is called the Global Synchronization Log (GSL).

Digital Asset has a notable contract to use DLT to modernise and replace the Australian Stock Exchange's technology systems, a major vote of confidence for Digital Asset and the entire private blockchain industry.

Hyperledger Fabric

Hyperledger Fabric was originally developed by IBM and Digital Asset and incubated under the Linux Foundation's Hyperledger Project. It has some traction in supply chains and healthcare.

JP Morgan Quorum

Quorum was created by US bank JP Morgan Chase and is based on the Ethereum platform. It uses advanced cryptographic techniques called zero-knowledge proofs to obfuscate transaction data. In March 2018, the *Financial Times* reported that JP Morgan was considering spinning off the project into its own entity.

Blockchain Experiments

Many experiments using blockchain technology have been announced by start-ups and incumbents alike. They are often described as "use cases," a term that implies that a blockchain would be a good use for the problem described. You can use a blockchain in almost any business situation that involves data. After all, a blockchain is a database with additional features.

It is still unclear which processes will be significantly improved as a direct consequence of the technology and which are improved simply by digitising the workflows.

In many cases a project might not need a blockchain, but using one might trigger management enthusiasm, possibly unlocking a budget not available to a boring digitisation project. Without some amount of interest, there would be less money to spend on innovating and therefore potentially less innovation.

Questions to Ask

Certain questions can be useful to ask. Earlier we asked, "Which blockchain?" and, "The public one or a private one?" From there, the questions depend on the answers to the original questions. Here are a few to get started.

For public blockchains, it is useful to understand:

- Will all parties run nodes or will some trust others?

- If the blockchain is backlogged, what impact might this have on users?

- How will the project deal with forks and chainsplits?

- How will data privacy be achieved?

- How will operators comply with evolving regulations?

For private blockchains, it is useful to understand:

- Who will run the nodes? Why?

- Who is going to write blocks?

- Who is going to validate blocks and why?

- If this is about data sharing, why can't a web server be used?

- Is there a natural central authority everyone trusts, and, if so, why aren't they hosting a portal?

For any type of blockchain:

- What data is represented on the blockchain and what data is "off-chain"?

- What do the tokens represent?

- When a token is passed from one party to another, what does this mean in real life?

- What happens if a private key is lost or copied? Is this acceptable?

- Are all parties comfortable with the data being passed around the network?

- How will upgrades be managed?

- What's in the blocks?

Depending on the project, some of these questions may be more relevant than others. Public chains can become congested, but payment channels may enable higher throughput. There are many more questions to ask, depending on the project.

At this stage of the innovation cycle, an honest "I don't know" is an acceptable answer for some of these questions, and it is more important to understand the trade-offs than to immediately pass judgment on the solutions.

Chapter 6

INITIAL COIN OFFERINGS

What Are ICOs?

Initial Coin Offerings (ICOs), sometimes called "token sales," are a new way for companies to raise money without diluting ownership of the company or having to pay back investors. According to icodata.io, over eleven billion US dollars were raised between 2014 and mid-2018 using some form of ICO. Early ICOs were Mastercoin (July 2013) and Maidsafe (July 2014) though they used the term "crowd sale." ICOs became popular in 2017.

Traditionally, a company can raise money through equity, debt, or pre-ordering of products. They can raise money from venture funding through a small number of investors, or from a large number, typically called "crowdfunding," which has become popular.

In an equity raise, investors pay money in return for a share of ownership of the company. In a debt raise, investors loan money to the company, expecting to get their capital back at the end of the lifetime of the loan. In a pre-fund or pre-order, customers (note, not investors) pay money for a product they will receive later, often not yet ready for distribution.

Crowdfunding uses the power of the internet, funding a project or company by raising small amounts of money from large numbers of people, often through a web or app-based platform. All types of funding can be raised from the "crowd." Equity crowdfunding platforms include Seedrs, AngelList, CircleUp, and Fundable. Debt crowdfunding platforms include Prosper, Lending Club, and Funding Circle. Pre-funding platforms include Kickstarter and IndieGoGo, where a project only succeeds if a target amount of money is pledged. Pre-ordering is popular for book and computer game sales.

Different ICOs have different characteristics. The industry is moving quickly, and regulators are starting to clarify their views on this new form of fundraising.

How Do ICOs Work?

Companies describe a product or service in a document called a whitepaper and announce their ICO. Investors send funds, usually cryptocurrencies, in return for tokens or tokens in the future. The tokens can represent anything but usually represent financial securities through the success of the project (called security tokens) or access to a product or service created by the venture (called utility tokens). At some stage, tokens may become listed on one or more cryptoasset exchanges. Eventually, a product or service is created, and in the case of utility tokens, holders may redeem their tokens for the product or service.

Whitepapers

According to Wikipedia, a white paper is an authoritative report or policy paper, originally used by the British government. The earliest well-known example was a 1922 paper commissioned by Winston Churchill, "Palestine. Correspondence with the Palestine Arab Delegation and the Zionist Organisation." The term *whitepaper* is no longer exclusively used for these documents.

Bitcoin's ideas were described in Satoshi Nakamoto's whitepaper. Ethereum was initially described in Vitalik Buterin's whitepaper, followed by a technical yellow paper written by Dr. Gavin Wood. Now, most ICO projects include a whitepaper, though lately resembling a less technical combination of a marketing document and investor prospectus.

Today's ICO whitepapers usually describe commercial, technical, and financial details of the project, including:

- The project's goal

- Milestone developments of the product or service

- The project team's background and experience

- The expected total fundraise value

- How the funds will be managed

- The purpose and use of the tokens

- The initial and ongoing distribution of the tokens

You can see some examples of ICO whitepapers on whitepaperdatabase.com, though note that inclusion in that website doesn't mean legitimacy of the project.

The Token Sale

Although ICOs operate differently, two routes emerged for token sale: a conservative route for tokens likely to be classified as securities in relevant jurisdictions and another route for tokens not likely to fall under securities regulations.

Projects whose tokens possibly fall under securities regulations fundraise in a traditional way. They might only advertise their tokens to rich people or those with experience in higher-risk financial instruments. In the USA, these investors are called "accredited investors" and other jurisdictions use "sophisticated investors" or similar terminology. Accredited investors are self-declared, and the criteria are based on net worth, annual income, and experience in complex financial instruments. Some ICOs will not sell tokens to American citizens or people living in certain countries. These ICOs will have private sales but no public sales or pre-sales, at least until the project has delivered a product and the tokens could be redefined as utility tokens.

Projects selling tokens likely to be classified as non-securities have more freedom to sell their tokens to a global audience and usually have a private sale, pre-sales, and a public sale.

Usually, projects offer discounts or bonuses to encourage investors to invest, with better deals for those participating in earlier rounds. Early Ethereum investors received 2,000 ETH per BTC, whereas later investors received only 1,337 ETH per BTC.

Funding rounds for start-up companies are similar, though the time scales and investor demands are different. ICOs can go from the first funding round to having their tokens listed on a cryptocurrency exchange in months with no product or commercial traction, whereas a traditional start-up usually takes years, and investors require demonstrable commercial success or potential.

ICO Funding Stages

Private Sales

In private sales, the investments, discounts, and bonuses are negotiated bilaterally between the project and each investor, like a traditional start-up raising funding.

A popular contract template is the Simple Agreement for Future Tokens, or SAFT, devised by digital currency lawyer Marco Santori among others, in an effort toward industry self-regulation. The SAFT is an agreement modelled on a Simple Agreement for Future Equity. An investor pays money now and will receive tokens later. The SAFT is a type of convertible note or a forward contract. The SAFT is a financial security, irrespective of the classification of the token.

Public Token Sales

Public sales are avoided by tokens that may be classified as security. However, they are still popular with some projects due to their global reach and ease of fundraising.

The project usually creates an Ethereum smart contract for receiving funds and displays the address on its website. Investors send money to the smart contract and receive tokens in a process automated by the smart contract.

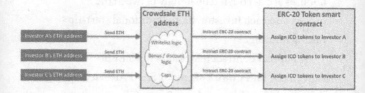

For some projects, the tokens may be ERC-20 compliant tokens recorded on the Ethereum blockchain. For others, especially projects creating new blockchain platforms, the tokens may be initially recorded as ERC-20 tokens on Ethereum to be redeemed later for tokens on the new blockchain when the new blockchain is up and running.

Ethereum's crowd sale accepted bitcoins as the funding currency and the Bitcoin address used was 36PrZ1KHYMpqSyAQXSG8VwbUiq2EogxLo2.

Public sales tend to be well-hyped. Countdowns and widgets displaying amounts raised are popular and often displayed prominently on the project's website. Social media, chat rooms, and bulletin boards are used to promote upcoming public sales.

Token Pre-Sales

Pre-sales are the "sale before the public sale," usually at a discounted price per token or with bonuses depending on the amount invested. They encourage investors to invest and form part of the hype for an ICO. An over-subscribed pre-sale is a great draw for investors in the main public sale.

Whitelisting

Both public sales and pre-sales may have some address "whitelisting" as part of a project's efforts to identify their investors. Before the token sale, potential investors click through a series of web pages, declare their identity information, perhaps upload a picture of their passport, accept terms and conditions, and provide the cryptocurrency address they intend to send funds from. During the actual token sale, the smart contract receiving funds will only accept funds from those cryptocurrency addresses that have been whitelisted.

Funding Caps

ICOs will declare funding caps in their whitepapers.
A soft cap usually represents the minimum amount
of funds needed for the project to go ahead (like
Kickstarter's "funding goal"), and a hard cap usually
represents the maximum the project will accept. Not
every ICO will have a hard or soft cap, and some may
change them according to demand.

Treasury

Projects will often create more tokens than are sold in
token sales in reserve. These reserves may be used to
reward founders, pay staff or contractors, or stabilise
the price of the tokens on exchanges. The project
may self-impose limits on how fast the reserves can
be spent, which offers investors confidence that the
project will not sell many tokens held in treasury
immediately after a sale and cause downward pressure
on the price.

Once a token is listed, the project will have some
idea of the token's value in its treasury. In accounting
terminology, these tokens are held on the company's
balance sheet, and so they impact the company's

equity valuation. Shareholders may like ICOs because they can create value on the company's balance sheet out of nothing.

Exchange Listing

Some investors may buy tokens at ICO to use the eventual product, service, or blockchain, but often investors want to make money by selling the tokens at a higher price than they bought them for.

Although tokens are immediately transferable between people once they are assigned to investors, listing the token on cryptoasset exchanges is a key event in the lifetime of an ICO because exchanges make the tokens more liquid. The transferability of the token makes the token different from the rewards-based crowdfunding, such as Kickstarter, where participants cannot easily resell their rewards to others.

If the project is popular, the listing can create an opportunity for new investors to accumulate the tokens, causing a rapid price increase. If the project is unpopular, early investors may use the listing as an opportunity to sell their tokens, causing a rapid fall in price.

Token listings are such an important event in the project that exchanges can charge projects, and listing fees of over a million US dollars are not uncommon. When a token is listed, the project will monitor the price carefully, and some have strategies of buying tokens back when the price is low.

Investors prefer to see a token listed on multiple reputable exchanges with large numbers of customers and lots of liquidity.

Despite the importance of exchange listing, projects tend to avoid discussing exchange listing timelines, especially those trying to keep their tokens from being classified as securities. Discussion of exchange listing adds weight to the classification of the token as a security since there is more of an expectation of profit from investors.

Traditional stock exchanges impose requirements on the companies they list, yet cryptoasset exchanges usually do not have such listing requirements, nor are they obligated to do so. Some cryptocurrency exchanges are happy to list any token, even those with a low likelihood of success (known colloquially as "shitcoins"), because the exchanges make revenues from trading fees. The exchanges make money as long as there is price volatility.

When Is a Token a Security?

Classifying a token as a security is important, because activities relating to financial securities are regulated in most countries. Note that tokens themselves are not regulated, but activities relating to them are.

In the USA, the "Howey Test" is a well-known test created by the United States Supreme Court in 1946 during *SEC v. Howey*. According to the FindLaw website:

> In Howey, two Florida-based corporate defendants offered real estate contracts for tracts of land with citrus groves. The defendants offered buyers the option of leasing any purchased land back to the defendants, who would then tend to the land, and harvest, pool, and market the citrus. As most of the buyers were not farmers and did not have agricultural expertise, they were happy to lease the land back to the defendants.
>
> The SEC sued the defendants over these transactions, claiming that they broke the law by not filing a securities registration statement. The Supreme Court, in issuing its decision finding

that the defendants' leaseback agreement is a form of security, developed a landmark test for determining whether certain transactions are investment contracts (and thus subject to securities registration requirements). Under the Howey Test, a transaction is an investment contract if:

1. It is an investment of money

2. There is an expectation of profits from the investment

3. The investment of money is in a common enterprise

4. Any profit comes from the efforts of a promoter or third party

Although the Howey Test uses the term "money," later cases have expanded this to include investments of assets other than money.

Each token offering could be checked against the Howey Test to determine whether the tokens qualify as "investment contracts." If so, then under the Securities Act of 1933 and the Securities Exchange Act of 1934, those tokens are considered securities and so activities relating to them are subject to certain requirements in the USA.

In February 2018, the Swiss financial regulator FINMA issued guidelines, saying that tokens can fall into one or more of the following categories, described below:

- **Payment tokens** are synonymous with cryptocurrencies and have no further functions or links to other development projects.

- **Utility tokens** are tokens intended to provide digital access to an application or service.

- **Asset tokens** represent assets such as real physical underlyings, companies, earnings streams, or an entitlement to dividends or interest payments.

FINMA suggests the following framework for determining whether a token is a financial security or not, and this seems reasonable in the current stage of industry development:

	Pre-financing and pre-sale / The token does not yet exist but the claims are tradeable	The token exists
ICO of payment tokens	$=$ Securities $\neq$ subject to AMLA	$\neq$ Securities $=$ means of payment under AMLA[3]
ICO of utility tokens[4]		$\neq$ Securities, if exclusively a functioning utility token $=$ Securities, if also or only investment function $\neq$ means of payment under AMLA if accessory
ICO of asset tokens[4]		$=$ Securities $\neq$ means of payment under AMLA

In June 2018, William Hinman, Director, Division of Corporate Finance at the United Stated Securities and Exchange Commission (SEC), said in a speech:

> Based on my understanding of the present state of Ether, the Ethereum network and its decentralized structure, current offers and sales of Ether are not securities transactions. And, as with Bitcoin, applying the disclosure regime of the federal securities laws to current transactions in Ether would seem to add little value.

He differentiates the way something (a token) is originally sold and the later use and sale of the token. A token can have utility and be offered as an investment contract, i.e., a financial security. He explains:

> The oranges in Howey had utility. Or in my favorite example, the Commission warned in the late 1960s about investment contracts sold in the form of whisky warehouse receipts. Promoters sold the receipts to US investors to finance the aging and blending processes of Scotch whisky. The whisky was real—and, for some, had exquisite utility. But Howey was not selling oranges and the warehouse receipts promoters were not selling whisky for consumption. They were selling investments, and the purchasers were expecting a return from the promoters' efforts.

This means that the way it is offered and the token's utility at the time of offering is important. We will see over the coming years how this important speech impacts the way ICOs are conducted.

Conclusion

Although we are in the early stages of the token industry, we can see that it is already beginning to mature.

In early ICOs, projects would write disclaimers in small print, stating the tokens are not an investment or a security, hoping that this would be enough to protect them. The projects sometimes described these investment rounds as "donations" or "contribution rounds" to disassociate with legally sensitive terminology. There was a clear disconnect between investor expectations of the tokens and the wording in the investor documents. Unfortunately, wording matters less than the economic realities, as projects are finding out.

In 2017, there was a wave of attempts to self-regulate and create industry standards. Projects trying to do the right thing looked for regulatory clarity. Today, the amount of money at stake is significant, and regulators and policymakers are paying attention. Regulatory clarity can attract investment and allow projects to focus on business rather than legal uncertainty.

Regulators are now clarifying what they will and won't accept, and projects are moving to comply with or avoid regulation. The economics of tokens, or tokenomics, are yet to be fully described or understood.

Chapter 7

INVESTING

In this section are some considerations to help you decide whether investing in cryptoassets is right for you. The markets are exciting, and people have made and lost fortunes in these markets.

Pricing

How do you put a value on cryptocurrencies or cryptoassets? For tokens that are a claim on an underlying asset, such as one ounce of gold, the price of the token should track the price of the underlying asset. However, cryptocurrencies are not a claim on any asset or backed by an entity. Is there a way to calculate a fair value for them?

We can ask three independent questions:

1. What is the current price of the cryptoasset?
2. What causes prices to change?
3. What should the price be?

What Is the Current Price of the Cryptoasset?

The market determines the current price of any asset. Cryptoassets trade on one or more exchanges, and prices and liquidity can differ between exchanges. Exchanges that report the most trade volume provide a good measure of the price, as they are the most active and should have the most liquidity.

Coinmarketcap.com provides data about the current price of tokens and which exchanges they trade on. If you click on the name of a token and then click on "Markets," you can see where that token trades and how much volume the exchange says it has traded.

What Causes Prices to Change?

The prices of cryptocurrencies and tokens behave like any other financial asset, driven by buyers and sellers making trading decisions based on various factors:

1. Sentiment (how traders feel about the asset)

2. Gossip and chatter on forums and social media sites

3. Technical successes (e.g., when blockchains successfully implement technical upgrades that make them more useful or when an ICO makes progress on its roadmap)

4.   Technical failures (e.g., if transactions slow down or a weakness is found in the way the blockchain operates)

5.   Celebrity endorsements (e.g., Paris Hilton's endorsement of LydianCoin in September 2017 or John MacAfee's occasional promotional tweets)

6.   Founders getting arrested (e.g., when the founders of Centra token were arrested in the USA, and the price of the tokens fell by 60 percent)

7.   Orchestrated Pump & Dumps where people coordinate to all buy a coin together to make the price go up and persuade others to buy it at a higher price, then sell the coins to unsuspecting new buyers

8.   Manipulation by large holders of any token

What Should the Price Be?

There have been several attempts to create models to find a fair value for cryptocurrencies and tokens. A common but flawed model for putting a value on a Bitcoin is the "if the money in gold went into Bitcoin" model:

*If x percent of the money in gold (or
other asset class) moved into Bitcoin,
a single Bitcoin should be worth $y.*

The argument is as follows: The total value of gold in
circulation is estimated at eight trillion US dollars.
Let's say 5 percent (though this can be anywhere from
0–100 percent) of the people holding gold sold their
gold for dollars; it would release a large amount of
money; in this case $400 billion. If that money were
used to buy bitcoins, the total value of bitcoins in
circulation, referred to as the "market cap," would
increase by $400 billion. So, this must increase
the price of each Bitcoin by $23.5k ($400 billion /
17 million).

But this logic is wrong. The "money going into
Bitcoin" doesn't simply drop into the "market cap."
The reason is simple: When you buy $10,000 worth of
Bitcoin, someone else sells those bitcoins for $10,000.
The only thing that happens when you buy a Bitcoin
is that the Bitcoin changes ownership and some
cash changes ownership. There is no mathematical
relationship between how much money you spend
buying bitcoins from someone else and Bitcoin's
market cap.

Let's say the last price paid for BTC was $10,000. So the "market cap" of Bitcoin, assuming seventeen million Bitcoin outstanding, is: $10,000 x 17 million = $170,000,000,000 ($170 billion).

Now, let's say you want to buy a tiny amount of BTC (say ten dollars' worth), and the best price you can see is $10,002. So you pay ten dollars and buy 0.0009998 BTC (ten dollars divided by $10,002 per Bitcoin). The "market cap" is now: $10,002 x 17 million = $170,034,000,000, a difference of $34 million.

You didn't "pump in" thirty-four million dollars, but the market cap increased by that amount. So clearly the earlier argument is wrong.

Having said that, if there are more buyers with a greater desire to buy and pay whatever it takes to accumulate BTC, then the prices will increase. Likewise, if sellers sell bitcoins at any price, then prices will fall.

I also hear variations on the "cost of creation" argument. The price of Bitcoin should be at least the cost of mining them, and as difficulty increases, it costs more to mine bitcoins, so the price should rise. Alas, this is also false. The cost incurred by a miner bears no relation to the market price of Bitcoin. The price of Bitcoin affects the profitability of miners. If a miner is unprofitable, they will eventually stop mining, but this doesn't affect the price of bitcoins. If it costs me five thousand to dig up one ounce of gold, this doesn't mean the price of gold should be at least five thousand dollars an ounce. User ihrhase explains this with salmon and sauerkraut smoothies in a forum post in 2010:

Re: New exchange (Bitcoin Market)

I have to agree with MH, on his post from the other thread, BC will not have a real value until people are trading in BC, if you attempt to value it by trade from BC to $ and vice versa, all someone has to do to completely destroy your market is dump all BC for $.

If the BC marketplace cannot provide real-world goods and services for BC, then it will be doomed to failure…

Some people are stuck on the idea that BC is valued at the expense for generating BCs…

BUT…

The problem is that if there is no commodity available that people want, one cannot expect to see people pay $ for BC, regardless of the cost one incurs in generating them…

> It is like saying I spent $X on creating Salmon and
> Sauerkraut Smoothies, so people should buy it for
> $X, but since no one wants Salmon and Sauerkraut
> Smoothies, no one will buy them, most likely they
> will not take them for free.

Unfortunately, I have not yet found a reasonable, fair value model for cryptocurrencies.

ICO tokens should be easier to price. These tokens are redeemable for a good or service in the future, so putting a price on the token should be a case of figuring out what that good or service is worth. Right?

The fact is that ICOs who issue tokens want the price of their tokens to go up, as do their investors. For example, they say, "Tokens will allow you access to cloud storage," rather than, "One token will give you ten GB of cloud storage for one year starting in 2020." This is a deliberate strategy. If the issuers quantified the goods or services, constraining the price, preventing the token's price from massively increasing (what ICO issuers and investors want). I have never seen an ICO whitepaper quantify exactly what a token will be redeemable for.

Who Controls the Price of Utility Tokens?

Initially, the number of goods/services that the tokens can buy is unspecified, so the price of the token is subject to normal cryptocurrency market forces, and there is no way to do fundamental analysis on what a fair market price should be (you can't price "cloud storage" without quantifying how much, for how long). During this period, some ICOs influence the price of their tokens by buying them up when the price falls. Some ICOs even discuss this strategy in their whitepapers. ICOs often retain many tokens in their treasury, so they can sell some if the price rallies too aggressively. Essentially, they may act like a central bank of their tokens, managing the price.

Later, there comes the point when the project must make a decision: Do they set prices in fiat or tokens? Should one GB of cloud storage for one year cost ten dollars, payable in tokens at market rate, or should one GB of cloud storage for one year cost one token?

Let's explore the options.

1) Priced in Fiat, Paid in Tokens

If this is the case, then at first, you'd think that the price of tokens should be irrelevant. Customers hold fiat, then when they want to use the service, they buy the tokens and quickly redeem them.

As tokens are redeemed against the issuer, fewer and fewer of them exist in circulation unless the project reissues them and sells them for fiat to pay their staff. Fewer tokens may mean a higher price due to scarcity. So a project not reliant on reselling redeemed tokens to pay their costs can allow tokens to become more scarce over time. But a project that needs to keep reselling its tokens to cover its costs will not. The company's financial health may impact the token's pricing pressures.

2) Priced in Tokens, Paid in Tokens

If the company sets the price of the goods or services in tokens, it will have control over the value of its tokens. Imagine that a competitor sells a similar product for ten dollars. If the project wants its tokens to be worth ten dollars, they set their product at a price of one token. If they want its tokens to be worth twenty dollars, they set their product at 0.5 tokens.

The competitor's pricing helps to peg the token's price. But, as they do this, their liabilities change. Their liabilities are the outstanding tokens in circulation, and by changing the price of one product from one token to 0.5 tokens, existing token holders can redeem tokens for twice as many products.

If the company decides to price its product in tokens, are tokens a good investment? Probably. The founders of the project, provided they haven't done a quick exit scam, also hold tokens and are financially incentivised to keep the price of tokens high.

So, projects have more control over their token price if they price their services in tokens, and I would expect that, as projects come to maturity, we will see projects priced in tokens, providing that the projects haven't been shut down for violating securities regulations first.

Risks and Mitigations

Market Risk

Cryptoasset prices are volatile, and many have fallen to zero. At the time of writing, deadcoins.com lists over eight hundred coins which have met that fate. Even popular cryptocurrencies after time, a significant hack, or exploited vulnerability could cause a fatal loss of confidence in the asset at any time.

Liquidity Risk

Liquidity risk is when the market cannot support your transaction at the expected price. Less popular coins are less liquid, meaning a large buy or sell can move the market against you more than expected.

With less popular coins or coins of regulatory uncertainty, there is also a risk that they are de-listed by exchanges, reducing their liquidity. In May 2018, Poloniex announced they were de-listing seventeen tokens.

Exchange Risks

It is convenient to keep assets on exchanges. You don't need private keys and can quickly trade between assets. However, exchanges have had an extremely poor track record of securing customer assets. Michael Matthews published a list of a selection of cryptocurrency exchange hacks between 2012 and 2016:

Date	Bitcoin Service Targeted	Attack Details	BTC Stolen	USD Value
2016 Aug	Bitfinex (exchange)	user wallets/ inside job	119,756	$66,000,000
2016 May	Gatecoin (exchange)	hot wallet	multicurrency	$2,000,000
2016 Mar	ShapeShift (exchange)	inside job	multicurrency	$230,000
2016 Mar	Cointrader	hot wallet	81 BTC	$33,600
2016 Jan	Bitstamp (exchange)	hot wallet	18,866	$5,263,614
2015 Feb	Bter (exchange)	cold wallet/inside job	7,000	$1,750,000
2015 Feb	Exco.in (exchange)	cold wallet/inside job	n/a	n/a
2015 Feb	Kipcoin (exchange)	cold wallet/inside job	3,000	$690,000
2015 Feb	796 (exchange)	cold wallet/inside job	1,000	$230,000
2015 Jan	Bitstamp (exchange)	hot wallet 1	19,000	$5,100,000
2015 Jan	Cavirtex (exchange)	user database stolen	n/a	n/a

2014 Dec	Blockchain.info (wallet)	user wallets (bug, R values)	267	$101,000
2014 Dec	Mintpal (exchange)	inside job	3,700	$3,208,412
2014 Aug	Cryptsy (exchange)	inside job	multicurrency	$6,000,000
2014 Mar	Flexcoin (wallet)	hot wallet	1,000	$738,240
2014 Mar	CryptoRush (exchange)	cold wallet/inside job	950	$782,641
2014 Jan	Mt.gox (exchange)	hot & cold wallets/ inside job	850,000	$700,258,171
2013 Dec	Blockchain.info (wallet)	two-factor authentication breach	800	$800,000
2013 Nov	Inputs.io (wallet)	cold wallet/inside job	4,100	$4,370,000
2013 Nov	BIPS (wallet)	cold wallet/inside job	1,200	$1,200,000
2012 Mar	Linode (webhosting)	inside job	46,703	$228,845

Not only have exchanges been successfully hacked by external parties, but it is not unknown for staff at exchanges to steal cryptocurrencies from their customers.

Being hacked is an existential threat to exchanges. So the top exchanges take security extremely seriously. Nevertheless, you should only keep as much on an exchange as you are willing to lose.

Exchanges and users of exchanges may also engage in illegal or unethical activity. Tricks borrowed from the wholesale financial markets industry include:

- Painting the tape: Artificially increasing trading activity by having parties controlled by the exchange repeatedly trade with each other.

- Spoofing: Submitting orders with the intention of cancelling them before they are matched.

- Front-running: An exchange can see a customer order and use the information to trade before the customer's order is accepted.

- Running stops: "stop loss" orders are not visible to other exchange customers but are visible to the exchange. Insiders can use this information to trade against their customers.

- Fake liquidity: Exchanges can publish "unfillable" orders that disappear or only partially fill when a customer tries to match them. This makes it look like there is more liquidity on the exchange than there is.

Different exchanges behave with different levels of professionalism. Many exchanges are dodgy. Do your research.

Wallet Risks

With wallets, there is a trade-off between security and convenience. Online wallets on computers or smartphones are easier to make cryptocurrency payments from. However, storing private keys on a device exposed to the internet is not advised.

In the past, it was common for people to print private keys onto bits of paper, but this is troublesome for making payments. Now, hardware wallets are the best compromise between security and convenience. Many wallets open source their code to allow developers and security professionals to understand exactly how the wallet works and assure them that there are no weaknesses, but this also provides transparency to hackers.

Regulatory Risks

Regulation around cryptocurrencies and tokens is evolving. ICOs are operating in a legal grey area in many jurisdictions, and there is a risk that some are deemed to have been illegally performing regulated activities.

Depending on the jurisdiction and classification of cryptoassets, and what you do with them, tax also needs to be considered.

Scams

Finally, due to the nature of the cryptocurrency industry, many scams operate. Some popular scams are:

- Ponzi schemes: Investors are promised good returns and old investors are paid with new investors' money.

- Exit scams: Founders of a project, wallet, exchange, or investment scheme run off with customer money.

- Fake hacks: Project gets hacked by an associate who shares profit with the project team.

- Pump & Dumps: Illiquid coins are bought
  cheaply by fraudsters then hyped on
  social media and sold at a higher price to
  new investors.

- Scam ICOs: ICO raises money with no
  intention of delivering a product. Sometimes
  listing well-known industry experts as
  advisors without the knowledge or approval of
  the expert.

- Spoof ICOs: Clones of real ICO websites made
  with the scammer's deposit address instead of
  the legitimate deposit address.

- Scam mining schemes: Claims investors
  will earn lots of cryptocurrencies, but key
  information such as difficulty increases is
  not disclosed.

- Fake wallets: Wallet software allows the
  scammer to access private keys, so the coins
  can be stolen from the user.

There are many variations to these, and scammers are
proving increasingly innovative.

People have made and lost fortunes trading
cryptocurrencies and investing in ICOs, but there

are many risks. If you decide to get involved, be careful and do a lot of research before committing your money.

CONCLUSION

In this book, I set out to explain the basics of bitcoins and blockchains, and I hope that it has been easy to follow. At the least, I have provided some ideas about concepts and terms for you to research further and perhaps ignited a curiosity that you may not have had before.

It is important to understand the blockchain industry, including cryptocurrencies, business blockchains, and tokenization of assets is in its infancy. Two important things have been created:

1. New censorship-resistant financial assets, methods of value transfer, and transparent automation

2. New technologies for business-to-business data and asset transfer

We can call these, respectively, a "crypto" story and a "blockchain" story.

The Crypto Story

Public blockchains are creating a new wave of censorship-resistant digital assets and unstoppable automated computations. For the first time in history, people can transfer value electronically worldwide without needing third parties to approve the transaction. Payments can be sent to smart contracts that guarantee certain outcomes without manual steps.

The Blockchain Story

Businesses are investing in private and public blockchains to reduce costs and risks, increase revenues, or create new business models. Private blockchains are rapidly evolving and improving. These multi-party database systems promise to remove duplicative processes and allow digital assets and records to move freely between businesses without intermediaries.

The Future

In the public cryptocurrency industry, innovation will continue to accelerate as tokens create financial

incentives that attract developers and other staff.
Many developers personally hold cryptocurrencies
and tokens and are financially incentivised to make
their projects successful.

Computer game items are a good candidate for
tokenizing assets, products, and services. Imagine
owning the unique sword a famous gamer used to
defeat an opponent. Imagine owning the signed digital
football used in an e-sports World Cup final. E-sports
and cryptoassets are a trend, not a fad, and it would be
unwise to bet against them.

ICOs will continue to be popular, and the industry
will begin to standardise with best practices and
common investor expectations. Regulations will
become more clear, and this will enable those currently
on the sidelines to participate.

Whether bitcoins, Ether, and other
cryptocurrencies become more price-stable, we will
see cryptoassets with a stable price with respect to
fiat currencies. Fiat currency will be tokenized and
recorded on blockchains. Whether these crypto-
fiat tokens are best issued by banks, e-money
businesses, or somehow by smart contracts is still to
be determined. Stable cryptoassets will enable another
cycle of innovation.

However, in recent years both Bitcoin and Ethereum have had periods of stress where miners couldn't process transactions quickly enough, causing backlogs. Engineers are working on solutions to these problems, and concepts such as sharding and state channels can allow public blockchains to scale.

Forks and chainsplits will become more problematic due to the confusion that they create. Proof-of-work is energy intensive and is polluting the planet. Ethereum may move to proof-of-stake, a much less energy-intensive block-writing mechanism, and if successful, other blockchains may follow suit.

As the value recorded on blockchains increases, governance will become increasingly important. A public ledger called Hadera Hashgraph is experimenting with having a formal governance structure over a public and accessible distributed ledger.

Business will adopt private blockchains, and then sooner or later, they will come together to form larger networks, just as the internet was formed from individual private networks.

Assets and records represented digitally will change ownership at the speed of email with fewer steps and costs. We will learn how to use this technology to move documents across organisational boundaries. These documents are assets that can all be represented as tokens on distributed ledgers, with much stronger authenticity guarantees due to the use of digital signatures. Many digital documents should only be represented once, with the right parties having visibility into the latest version.

Whether between or within organisations, when data sets need to be passed from one system to another, the receiving system needs to be confident that the data hasn't been corrupted. This situation happens a lot in banking—often huge lists of trades need to be sent from one system to another. Trades can be recorded and sent with a hash to a previous trade in the set, and then the receiving system can know that the complete set of trades has not been altered by accident or malice.

In the future, it will make little sense to manage any document or data set that needs to cross organisational boundaries using anything other than a blockchain.

These improvements will increase the velocity of business done within countries and across borders. This has a huge impact not only for the financial services industry but also for the real economy.

Smart contracts will enable business-to-business automation in a guaranteed way that hasn't been possible before.

Automation has tended to stop at the boundaries of businesses, with each business double-checking the other. With smart contracts, these rules can be automated and validated automatically.

Blockchains enable atomic transactions, transactions that make multiple changes to the ledger simultaneously or not at all. Atomic, because the changes are bundled together and indivisible. On a blockchain, an atomic transaction can be created that includes both changes of ownership. That transaction is committed entirely, and either succeeds as a whole or fails. In finance this concept is called "delivery versus payment." Blockchain technology now provides the technological means to do this.

At first, private blockchains will be used to do the same business as today but better, faster, and cheaper. Later, there will be a shift, and industries will start to evolve their processes. Once necessary, intermediaries will be made irrelevant, driving down transaction costs.

The financial services industry is particularly at risk of disruption from this technology. Before blockchains, third-party intermediaries were needed to keep track of digital assets. You've never been able to digitally own and directly control a financial asset. Third parties keep track of who owns what, and it is their job to prevent double-spending. However, with cryptoassets, you can hold and control your assets, though this has its risks. The blockchain will result in fewer intermediaries, meaning fewer businesses that extract profit from the real economy.

There is a possibility that the distinction between public and private blockchains fades away or that assets can jump between one blockchain and another with such ease that the blockchains become a matter of preference and matter as little as which device you use to check your email.

We have already seen the start of disintermediation. In ICOs, huge sums of money are being transferred around the world without a bank in sight. In June 2016, I helped arrange the custody of almost 25,000 bitcoins seized as proceeds of crime, worth sixteen million Australian dollars at the time. The bitcoins were held in custody by EY, a professional services firm, for a month before being transferred to winners of a global auction. No bank needed to be paid.

Whether you are a proponent of blockchains, believe in the long-term viability of cryptocurrencies, or think that decentralisation is a good thing, this industry is certainly delivering change. Whether these tools will be used for good or bad depends on how the technology is adopted, by whom, and for what purpose.

Appendix

THE FED

The Federal Reserve is not a single central bank. It is a central banking system. The system is comprised of three main parts: twelve regional Federal Reserve banks, the Federal Reserve Board, and the Federal Open Market Committee (FOMC). According to Wikipedia:

> *The Federal Reserve System is composed of several layers. It is governed by the presidentially appointed Board of Governors or Federal Reserve Board (FRB). Twelve regional Federal Reserve Banks, located in cities throughout the nation, oversee the privately-owned US member banks. Nationally chartered commercial banks are required to hold stock in the Federal Reserve Bank of their region, which entitles them to elect some of their board members. The FOMC sets monetary policy; it consists of all seven members of the Board of Governors and the twelve regional bank presidents, though only five bank presidents vote at any given time: the president of the New York Fed and four others who rotate through one-year terms.*

When people talk about the "big" Fed, they are usually talking about either the Board of Governors of the Federal Reserve System ("The Board of Governors") or the FOMC. The "little" Feds are the twelve regional Federal Reserve Banks.

Board of Governors

According to the St. Louis Fed, the Board of Governors guides the Federal Reserve's policy actions and consists of up to seven governors, appointed by the president of the United States and confirmed by the Senate. As of June 2018, three governors guide the Fed.

Federal Open Market Committee

The FOMC is the body that raises or lowers interest rates. The St. Louis Fed describes the committee as:

> *...the Fed's chief body for monetary*
> *policy. Its voting membership combines*
> *the seven members of the Board of*
> *Governors, the president of the Federal*
> *Reserve Bank of New York, and four other*
> *Reserve Bank presidents, who serve*
> *one-year terms on a rotating basis with*
> *the other Reserve Bank presidents.*

According to the Chicago Fed:

> *The monetary policy goals of the Federal*
> *Reserve are to foster economic conditions*
> *that achieve both stable prices and*
> *maximum sustainable employment.*

The target goal for the FOMC is to set monetary policy to create a 2 percent per year CPI. 2 percent seems small but has a significant effect over a lifetime. The maximum stable employment rate is targeted at 95.4 percent employment, or 4.6 percent unemployment.

The FOMC oversees and sets policy on open market operations, the principal tool of national monetary policy. The committee meets eight times a year, approximately once every six weeks. As of June

2018, out of a maximum of twelve voting members, only eight committee members were appointed.

Little Fed

The "Little Feds" are the twelve separately incorporated regional Federal Reserve Banks (regional FRBs). They are based in the cities of Boston, New York, Philadelphia, Cleveland, Richmond, Atlanta, Chicago, St. Louis, Minneapolis, Kansas City, Dallas, and San Francisco.

The regional FRBs are responsible for supervising and examining state member banks, lending to depository institutions, providing key financial services (e.g., interbank payment systems), and examining certain financial institutions. They also provide the US government with a ready source of loans and serve as the safe depository for federal money.

The regional FRBs are not part of the federal government of the USA but are set up like private corporations, according to the St. Louis Fed. The shareholders are banks from the private banking sector who receive a tax-free 6 percent dividend from the regional FRBs in any year that the regional FRB makes money. In fact, nationally chartered banks must purchase some amount of this stock, with the amount based on their size. It is nice to be a bank and be forced to own the central bank and receive guaranteed dividends risk-free!

ACKNOWLEDGMENTS

This book would not have been possible without the support of many people.

Along this journey, and although I may not agree with all of them all the time, I have been influenced by people with a wide range of perspectives. I am grateful to them for sharing their knowledge and opinions with the world. I have particularly enjoyed content from Gavin Andresen, Andreas Antonopoulos, Richard Gendal Brown, Vitalik Buterin, Gideon Greenspan, Ian Grigg, Dave Hudson, Izabella Kaminska, Rusty Russell, Tim Swanson, Robert Sams, Emin Gun Sirer, and Angela Walch.

Other friends have been generous with their time and expertise: Drew Graham and Varun Mittal have been at the end of WhatsApp, responding quickly when I have needed help or inspiration, and industry experts in various crypto-related chat rooms have consistently made themselves instantly available to

contribute with a quick insult or flippant comment—
thank you.

I am immensely grateful to the team at Mango
Publishing for their work in making this book a
reality: Ashley, Hannah, Mario, Michelle, Natasha,
Roberto, Chris, and the others working behind the
scenes. Thank you, Hugo, for taking a risk and having
confidence in me.

Sarah, thank you for looking after our children
while I sat for many hours writing in coffee shops
and occasionally reminding me of my real-life
responsibilities as husband and father too.

Finally, I'd like to thank my father, Kevin, who
spent many hours diligently editing my drafts despite
having minimal prior interest or experience in
cryptocurrencies! Papa, you are now a Bitcoin expert.

It takes a decentralised village to raise a book
on cryptocurrencies.

ABOUT THE AUTHOR

Inspired by a Bitcoin conference in 2013, Antony left a conventional banking career in Singapore to join a little start-up called itBit. A Bitcoin exchange, itBit is a website where clients can buy and sell bitcoins and was one of the first waves of venture capital funded companies in the nascent cryptocurrency industry.

In 2015, after itBit raised another round of venture funding and moved its headquarters to New York, Antony left and privately consulted with clients, writing papers and running workshops to explain this new technology to curious professionals.

In 2016, Antony joined R3, a financial industry consortium created to collaboratively explore the benefits of blockchain technology. As director of research, he explains the evolving concepts and technologies to clients, policymakers, and the public.

Before becoming obsessed with bitcoins and blockchains, Antony was a technologist at Credit Suisse in London and Singapore, having started his banking career as an FX spot trader at Barclays Capital in 2007.

Antony studied natural sciences at Gonville & Caius College, Cambridge University, where he gained two full Blues for sailing and graduated in 2004 with a 2:1.

Antony lives in Singapore with his wife Sarah and their two children. He tweets from @antony_btc and blogs at www. bitsonblocks.net.

Mango Publishing, established in 2014, publishes an eclectic list of books by diverse authors—both new and established voices—on topics ranging from business, personal growth, women's empowerment, LGBTQ studies, health, and spirituality to history, popular culture, time management, decluttering, lifestyle, mental wellness, aging, and sustainable living. We were recently named 2019 and 2020's #1 fastest growing independent publisher by Publishers Weekly. Our success is driven by our main goal, which is to publish high quality books that will entertain readers as well as make a positive difference in their lives.

Our readers are our most important resource; we value your input, suggestions, and ideas. We'd love to hear from you—after all, we are publishing books for you!

Please stay in touch with us and follow us at:

Facebook: Mango Publishing
Twitter: @MangoPublishing
Instagram: @MangoPublishing
LinkedIn: Mango Publishing
Pinterest: Mango Publishing

Newsletter: mangopublishinggroup.com/newsletter

Join us on Mango's journey to reinvent publishing, one book at a time.